Kristen Suzanne's
ULTIMATE
Raw Vegan
Hemp
Recipes

Fast & Easy Raw Food Hemp Recipes for Delicious Soups, Salads, Dressings, Bread, Crackers, Butter, Spreads, Dips, Breakfast, Lunch, Dinner & Desserts

by Kristen Suzanne

*Green
Butterfly
Press*

Scottsdale, Arizona

OTHER BOOKS BY KRISTEN SUZANNE

- *Kristen's Raw: The EASY Way to Get Started & Succeed at the Raw Food Vegan Diet & Lifestyle*
- *Kristen Suzanne's EASY Raw Vegan Entrees*
- *Kristen Suzanne's EASY Raw Vegan Desserts*
- *Kristen Suzanne's EASY Raw Vegan Soups*
- *Kristen Suzanne's EASY Raw Vegan Sides & Snacks*
- *Kristen Suzanne's EASY Raw Vegan Salads & Dressings*
- *Kristen Suzanne's EASY Raw Vegan Smoothies, Juices, Elixirs & Drinks (includes wine drinks!)*
- *Kristen Suzanne's EASY Raw Vegan Holidays*
- *Kristen Suzanne's EASY Raw Vegan Dehydrating*

COMING SOON

- *Kristen Suzanne's Raw Vegan Diet for EASY Weight Loss*
- *Kristen Suzanne's Ultimate Raw Vegan Chocolate Recipes*

For details, Raw Food resources, and Kristen's free Raw Food newsletter, please visit:

KristensRaw.com

For information on excerpting, reprinting or licensing portions of this book, please write to info@greenbutterflypress.com.

Green Butterfly Press
19550 N. Gray Hawk Drive, Suite 1042
Scottsdale, AZ 85255 USA

Library of Congress Control Number: 2009920147
Library of Congress Subject Heading:
1. Cookery (Natural foods) 2. Raw foods

ISBN: 978-0-9817556-9-4
1.3

CONTENTS

CHAPTER 1

RAW BASICS

NOTE: "Raw Basics" is a brief introduction to Raw for those who are new to the subject. It is the same in all of my recipe books. If you have recently read this section in one of them, you may wish to skip to Chapter 2.

WHY RAW?

Living the Raw vegan lifestyle has made me a more effective person... in everything I do. I get to experience pure, sustainable all-day-long energy. My body is in perfect shape and I gain strength and endurance in my exercise routine with each passing day. My relationships are the best they've ever been, because I'm happy and I love myself and my life. My headaches have ceased to exist, and my skin glows with the radiance of brand new life, which is exactly how I feel. Raw vegan is the best thing that has ever happened to me.

Whatever your passion is in life (family, business, exercise, meditation, hobbies, etc.), eating Raw vegan will take it to unbelievable new heights. Raw vegan food offers you the most amazing benefits – physically, mentally, and spiritually. It is *the* ideal choice for your food consumption if you want to become the healthiest and best "you" possible. Raw vegan food is for people who want to live longer while feeling younger. It's for people who want to feel vibrant and alive, and want to enjoy life like never before. All I ever have to say to someone is, "Just try it for yourself." It will change your life. From simple to gourmet, there's always something for everyone, and it's delicious. Come into the world of Raw with me, and experience for yourself the most amazing health *ever*.

Are you ready for your new lease on life? The time is now. Let's get started!

SOME GREAT THINGS TO KNOW BEFORE DIVING INTO THESE RECIPES

Organic Food

I use organic produce and products for pretty much everything. There are very few exceptions, and that would be if the recipe called for something I just can't get organic such as jicama, young Thai coconuts, certain seasonings, or any random ingredient that my local health food store is not able to procure from an organic grower for whatever reason.

If you think organic foods are too expensive, then start in baby steps and buy a few things at a time. Realize that you're going to be spending less money in the long run on health problems as your health improves, and going organic is one way to facilitate that. I find that once people learn about the direct cause-and-effect relationship between non-organic food and illnesses such as cancer, the relatively small premium you pay for organic becomes a trivial non-issue. Your health is worth it!

Choosing organically grown foods is one of the most important choices we can make. The more people who choose organic, the lower the prices will be in the long run. Vote with your dollar! Here is something I do to help further this cause and you can, too… whenever I eat at a restaurant I always write on the bill, "I would eat here more if you served organic food." Can you imagine what would happen if we all did this?

It's essential to use organic ingredients for many reasons:

1. The health benefits – superior nutrition, reduced intake of chemicals and heavy metals and decreased exposure to carcinogens. Organic food has been shown to have up to 300% more nutrition than conventionally grown, non-organic produce.

2. To have the very best tasting food ever! I've had people tell me in my classes that they never knew vegetables tasted so good – and it's because I only use organic.

3. Greater variety of heirloom fruits and vegetables.

4. Cleaner rivers and waterways for our earth, along with minimized topsoil erosion.

Going Organic on a Budget

Going organic on a budget is not impossible. Here are things to keep in mind that will help you afford it:

1. Buy in bulk. Ask the store you frequent if they'll give you a deal for buying certain foods by the case. (Just make sure it's a case of something that you can go through in a timely fashion so it doesn't go to waste). Consider this for bananas or greens especially if you drink lots of smoothies or green juice, like I do.

2. See if local neighbors, family or friends will share the price of getting cases of certain foods. When you do this, you can go beyond your local grocery store and contact great places (which deliver nationally) such as Boxed Greens (BoxedGreens.com) or Diamond Organics (DiamondOrganics.com). Maybe they'll extend a discount if your order goes above a certain amount or if you get certain foods by the case. It never hurts to ask.

3. Pay attention to organic foods that are not very expensive to buy relative to the conventional prices (bananas, for example). Load up on those.

4. Be smart when picking what you buy as organic. Some conventionally grown foods have higher levels of pesticides than others. For those, go organic. Then, for foods that are not sprayed as much, you can go conventional. Avocados, for example, aren't sprayed too heavily so you could buy those as conventional. Here is a resource that keeps an updated list: foodnews.org/walletguide.php

5. Buy produce that is on sale. Pay attention to which organic foods are on sale for the week and plan your menu around that. Every little bit adds up!

6. Grow your own sprouts. Load up on these for salads, soups, and smoothies. Very inexpensive. Buy the organic seeds in the bulk bins at your health food store or buy online and grow them yourself. Fun!

7. Buy organic seeds/nuts in bulk online and freeze. Nuts and seeds typically get less expensive when you order in bulk from somewhere like Sun Organic (SunOrganic.com). Take advantage of this and freeze

them (they'll last the year!). Do the same with dried fruits/dates/etc. And remember, when you make a recipe that calls for expensive nuts, you can often easily replace them with a less expensive seed such as sunflower or pumpkin seeds.

8. Buy seasonally; hence, don't buy a bunch of organic berries out of season (i.e., eat more apples and bananas in the fall and winter). Also, consider buying frozen organic fruits, especially when they're on sale!

9. Be content with minimal variety. Organic spinach banana smoothies are inexpensive. So, having this most mornings for your breakfast can save you money. You can change it up for fun by adding cinnamon one day, nutmeg another, vanilla extract yet another. Another inexpensive meal or snack is a spinach apple smoothie. Throw in a date or some raisins for extra pizazz. It helps the budget when you make salads, smoothies, and soups with ingredients that tend to be less expensive such as carrots (year round), bananas (year round), zucchini and cucumbers (in the summer), etc.

Kristen Suzanne's Tip: A Note About Herbs

Hands down, fresh herbs taste the best and have the highest nutritional value. While I recommend fresh herbs whenever possible, you can substitute dried herbs if necessary. But do so in a ratio of:

3 parts fresh to 1 part dried

Dried herbs impart a more concentrated flavor, which is why you need less of them. For instance, if your recipe calls for three tablespoons of fresh basil, you'll be fine if you use one tablespoon of dried basil instead.

The Infamous Salt Question: What Kind Do I Use?

All life on earth began in the oceans, so it's no surprise that organisms' cellular fluids chemically resemble sea water. Saltwater in the ocean is "salty" due to many, many minerals, not just sodium chloride. We need these minerals, not coincidentally, in roughly the same proportion that they exist in... guess where?... the ocean! (You've just gotta love Mother Nature.)

So when preparing food, I always use sea salt, which can be found at any health food store. Better still is sea salt that was deposited into salt beds before the industrial revolution started spewing toxins into the world's waterways. My personal preference is Himalayan Crystal Salt, fine granules. It's mined high in the mountains from ancient sea-beds, has a beautiful pink color, and imparts more than 84 essential minerals into your diet. You can use either the Himalayan crystal variety or Celtic Sea Salt, but I would highly recommend sticking to at least one of these two. You can buy Himalayan crystal salt through KristensRaw.com/store.

Kristen Suzanne's Tip: Start Small with Strong Flavors

FLAVORS AND THEIR STRENGTH

There are certain flavors and ingredients that are particularly strong, such as garlic, ginger, onion, and salt. It's important to observe patience here, as these are flavors that can be loved or considered offensive, depending on who is eating the food. I know people who want the maximum amount of salt called for in a recipe and I know some who are highly sensitive to it. Therefore, to make the best possible Raw experience for you, I recommend starting on the "small end" especially with ingredients like garlic, ginger, strong savory herbs and seasonings, onions (any variety), citrus, and even salt. If I've given you a range in a recipe, for instance *1/4 - 1/2 teaspoon Himalayan crystal salt* then I recommend starting with the smaller amount, and then tasting it. If you don't love it, then add a little more of that ingredient and taste it again. Start small. It's worth the extra 60 seconds it might take you to do this. You might end up using less, saving it for the next recipe you make and voila, you're saving a little money.

Lesson #1: It's very hard to correct any flavors of excess, so start small and build.

Lesson #2: Write it down. When an ingredient offers a "range" for itself, write down the amount you liked best. If you use an "optional" ingredient, make a note about that as well.

One more thing to know about some strong flavors like the ones mentioned above... with Raw food, these flavors can intensify the finished product as each day passes. For example, the garlic in your soup, on the day you made it, might be perfect. On day two, it's still really great but a little stronger in flavor. And by day three, you might want to carry around your toothbrush or a little chewing gum!

HERE IS A TIP TO HELP CONTROL THIS

If you're making a recipe in advance, such as a dressing or soup that you won't be eating until the following day or even the day after that, then hold off on adding some of the strong seasonings until the day you eat it (think garlic and ginger). Or, if you're going to make the dressing or soup in advance, use less of the strong seasoning, knowing that it might intensify on its own by the time you eat it. This isn't a huge deal because it doesn't change that dramatically, but I mention it so you won't be surprised, especially when serving a favorite dish to others.

Kristen Suzanne's Tip: Doubling Recipes

More often than not, there are certain ingredients and flavors that you don't typically double in their entirety, if you're making a double or triple batch of a recipe. These are strong-flavored ingredients similar to those mentioned above (salt, garlic, ginger, herbs, seasoning, etc). A good rule of thumb is this: For a double batch, use 1.5 times the amount for certain ingredients. Taste it and see if you need the rest. For instance, if I'm making a "double batch" of soup, and the normal recipe calls for 1 tablespoon of Himalayan crystal salt, then I'll put in 1 1/2 tablespoons to start, instead of two. Then, I'll taste it and add the remaining 1/2 tablespoon, if necessary.

This same principle is not necessarily followed when dividing a recipe in half. Go ahead and simply divide in half, or by whatever amount you're making. If there is a range for a particular ingredient provided, I still recommend that you use the smaller amount of an ingredient when dividing. Taste the final product and then decide whether or not to add more.

My recipes provide a variety of yields, as you'll see below. Some recipes make 2 servings and some make 4 - 6 servings. For those of you making food for only yourself, then simply cut the recipes making 4 - 6 servings in half. Or, as I always do... I make the larger serving size and then I have enough food for a couple of meals. If a recipe yields 2 servings, I usually double it for the same reason.

Kristen Suzanne's Tip: Changing Produce

"But I made it exactly like this last time! Why doesn't it taste the same?"

Here is something you need to embrace when preparing Raw vegan food. Fresh produce can vary in its composition of water, and even flavor, to some degree. There are times I've made marinara sauce and, to me, it was the perfect level of sweetness in the finished product. Then, the next time I made it, you would have thought I added a smidge of sweetener. This is due to the fact that fresh Raw produce can have a slightly different taste from time to time when you make a recipe (only ever so slightly, so don't be alarmed). *Aahhh, here is the silver lining!* This means you'll never get bored living the Raw vegan lifestyle because your recipes can change a little in flavor from time to time, even though you followed the same recipe. Embrace this natural aspect of produce and love it for everything that it is. ☺

This is much less of an issue with cooked food. Most of the water is taken out of cooked food, so you typically get the same flavors and experience each and every time. Boring!

Kristen Suzanne's Tip: Ripeness and Storage for Your Fresh Produce

1. I never use green bell peppers because they are not "ripe." This is why so many people have a hard time digesting them (often "belching" after eating them).

To truly experience the greatest health, it's important to eat fruits and vegetables at their peak ripeness. Therefore, make sure you only use red, orange, or yellow bell peppers. Store these in your refrigerator.

2. A truly ripe banana has some brown freckles or spots on the peel. This is when you're supposed to eat a banana. Store these on your countertop away from other produce, because bananas give off a gas as they ripen, which will affect the ripening process of your other produce. And, if you have a lot of bananas, split them up. This will help prevent all of your bananas from ripening at once.

3. Keep avocados on the counter until they reach ripeness (when their skin is usually brown in color and if you gently squeeze it, it "gives" just a little). At this point, you can put them in the refrigerator where they'll last up to a week longer. If you keep ripe avocados on the counter, they'll only last another couple of days. Avocados, like bananas, give off a gas as they ripen, which will affect the ripening process of your other produce. Let them ripen away from your other produce. And, if you have a lot of avocados, separate them. This will help prevent all of your avocados from ripening at once.

4. Tomatoes are best stored on your counter. Don't put them in the refrigerator or they'll get a "mealy" texture.

5. Pineapple is ripe for eating when you can gently pull a leaf out of the top of it. Therefore, test your pineapple for ripeness at the store to ensure you're buying the sweetest one possible. Just pull one of the

leaves out from the top. After 3 to 4 attempts on different leaves, if you can't gently take one of them out, then move on to another pineapple.

6.   Stone fruits (fruits with pits, such as peaches, plums, and nectarines), bananas and avocados all continue to ripen after being picked.

7.   I have produce ripening all over my house. Sounds silly maybe, but I don't want it crowded on my kitchen countertop. I move it around and turn it over daily.

For a more complete list of produce ripening tips, check out my book, *Kristen's Raw*, available at Amazon.com.

Kristen Suzanne's Tip: Proper Dehydration Techniques

Dehydrating your Raw vegan food at a low temperature is a technique that warms and dries the food while preserving its nutritional integrity. When using a dehydrator, it is recommended that you begin the dehydrating process at a temperature of 130 - 140 degrees for about an hour. Then, lower the temperature to 105 degrees for the remaining time of dehydration. Using a high temperature such as 140 degrees, *in the initial stages of dehydration*, does not destroy the nutritional value of the food. During this initial phase, the food does the most "sweating" (releasing moisture), which cools the food. Therefore, while the temperature of the air circulating *around* the food is about 140 degrees, the food itself is much cooler. These directions apply only when using an Excalibur Dehydrator because of their Horizontal-Airflow Drying System. Furthermore, I am happy to only recommend

Excalibur dehydrators because of their first-class products and customer service. For details, visit the *Raw Kitchen Essential Tools* section of my website at KristensRaw.com/store.

MY YIELD AND SERVING AMOUNTS NOTED IN THE RECIPES

Each recipe in this book shows an approximate amount that the recipe yields (the quantity it makes). I find that "one serving" to me might be considered two servings to someone else, or vice versa. Therefore, I tried to use an "average" when listing the serving amount. Don't let that stop you from eating a two-serving dish in one sitting, if it seems like the right amount for you. It simply depends on how hungry you are.

WHAT IS THE DIFFERENCE BETWEEN CHOPPED, DICED, AND MINCED?

Chop

This gives relatively uniform cuts, but doesn't need to be perfectly neat or even. You'll often be asked to chop something before putting it into a blender or food processor, which is why it doesn't have to be uniform size since it'll be getting blended or pureed.

Dice

This produces a nice cube shape, and can be different sizes, depending on which you prefer. This is great for vegetables.

Mince

This produces an even, very fine cut, typically used for fresh herbs, onions, garlic and ginger.

Julienne

This is a fancy term for long, rectangular cuts.

WHAT EQUIPMENT DO I NEED FOR MY NEW RAW FOOD KITCHEN?

I go into much more detail regarding the perfect setup for your Raw vegan kitchen in my book, *Kristen's Raw,* which is a must read for anybody who wants to learn the easy ways to succeed with living the Raw vegan lifestyle. Here are the main pieces of equipment you'll want to get you going:

1. An excellent chef's knife (6 - 8 inches in length – non-serrated). Of everything you do with Raw food, you'll be chopping and cutting the most, so invest in a great knife. This truly makes doing all the chopping really fun!

2. Blender

3. Food Processor (get a 7 or 10-cup or more)

4. Juicer

5. Spiralizer or Turning Slicer

6. Dehydrator – Excalibur® is the best company by far and is available at KristensRaw.com.)

7. Salad spinner

8. Other knives (paring, serrated)

For links to online retailers that sell my favorite kitchen tools and foods, visit KristensRaw.com/store.

SOAKING AND DEHYDRATING NUTS AND SEEDS

This is an important topic. When using nuts and seeds in Raw vegan foods, you'll find that recipes sometimes call for them to be "soaked" or "soaked and dehydrated." Here is the low-down on the importance and the difference between the two.

Why Should You Soak Your Nuts and Seeds?

Most nuts and seeds come packed by Mother Nature with enzyme inhibitors, rendering them harder to digest. These inhibitors essentially shut down the nuts' and seeds' metabolic activity, rendering them dormant – for as long as they need to be – until they detect a moisture-rich environment that's suitable for germination (e.g., rain). By soaking your nuts and seeds, you trick the nuts into "waking up," shutting off the inhibitors so that the enzymes can become active. This greatly enhances the nuts' digestibility for you and is highly recommended if you want to experience Raw vegan food in the healthiest way possible.

Even though you'll want to soak the nuts to activate their enzymes, before using them, you'll need to re-dry them and grind them down anywhere from coarse to fine (into a powder almost like flour), depending on the recipe. To dry them, you'll need a dehydrator. (If you don't own a dehydrator yet, then, if a recipe calls for "soaked and dehydrated," just skip the soaking part; you can use the nuts or seeds in the dry form that you bought them).

Drying your nuts (but not yet grinding them) is a great thing to do before storing them in the freezer or refrigerator (preferably in glass mason jars). They will last a long time and you'll always have them on hand, ready to use.

In my recipes, always use nuts and seeds that are "soaked and dehydrated" (that is, *dry*) unless otherwise stated as "soaked" (wet).

Some nuts and seeds don't have to follow the enzyme inhibitor rule; therefore, they don't need to be soaked. These are:

- Macadamia nuts
- Brazil nuts
- Pine nuts
- Hemp seeds
- Most cashews

An additional note... there are times when the recipe will call for soaking, even though it's for a type of nut or seed without enzyme inhibitors, such as Brazil nuts. The logic behind this is to help *soften* the nuts so they blend into a smoother texture, especially if you don't have a high-powered blender. This is helpful when making nut milks, soups and sauces.

Instructions for "Soaking" and "Soaking and Dehydrating" Nuts

"Soaking"

The general rule to follow: Any nuts or seeds that require soaking can be soaked overnight (6 - 10 hours). Put the required amount of nuts or seeds into a bowl and add enough water to cover by about an inch or so. Set them on your counter overnight. The following morning, or 6 - 10 hours after you soaked them, drain and rinse them. They are now ready to eat or use in a recipe. At this point, they need to be refrigerated in an airtight container (preferably a glass mason jar) and they'll have a shelf life of about 3 days maximum. Only soak the amount you're going to need or eat, unless you plan on dehydrating them right away.

A note about flax seeds and chia seeds... these don't need to be soaked if your recipe calls for grinding them into a powder. Some recipes will call to soak the seeds in their "whole-seed" form, before making crackers and bread, because they create a very gelatinous and binding texture when soaked. You can soak flax or chia seeds in a ratio of one-part seeds to two-parts water, and they can be soaked for as short as 1 hour and up to 12 hours. At this point, they are ready to use (don't drain them). Personally, when I use flax seeds, I usually grind them and don't soak them. It's hard for your body to digest "whole" flax seeds, even if they are soaked. It's much easier for your body to assimilate the nutrients when they're ground to a flax meal.

"Soaking and Dehydrating"

Follow the same directions for soaking. Then, after draining and rinsing the nuts, spread them out on a mesh dehydrator

16

sheet and dehydrate them at 140 degrees for one hour. Lower the temperature to 105 degrees and dehydrate them until they're completely dry, which can take up to 24 hours.

Please note, all nuts and seeds called for in my recipes will always be "Raw and Organic" and "Soaked and Dehydrated" unless the recipe calls for soaking.

ALMOND PULP

Some of my recipes call for "almond pulp," which is really easy to make. After making your fresh almond milk (see *Nut/Seed Milk* recipe, p. 25) and straining it through a "nut milk bag," (available at NaturalZing.com or you can use a paint strainer bag from the hardware store – much cheaper), you will find a nice, soft pulp inside the bag. Turn the bag inside out and flatten the pulp out onto a Paraflexx dehydrator sheet with a spatula or your hand. Dehydrate the pulp at 140 degrees for one hour, then lower the temperature to 105 degrees and continue dehydrating until the almond pulp is dry (up to 24 hours). Break the pulp into chunks and store in the freezer until you're ready to use it. Before using the almond pulp, grind it into a flour in your blender or food processor.

SOY LECITHIN

Some recipes (desserts, in particular) will call for soy lecithin, which is extracted from soybean oil. This optional ingredient is not Raw. If you use soy lecithin, I highly recommend using a brand that is "non-GMO," meaning it was processed without any genetically modified ingredients (a great brand is Health Alliance®). Soy lecithin helps your dessert (cheesecake, for example) maintain a firmer texture. That said, it's certainly not necessary. If an amount isn't suggested, a good rule of thumb is to use 1 teaspoon per 1 cup total recipe volume.

ICE CREAM FLAVORINGS

When making Raw vegan ice cream, it's better to use alcohol-free extracts so they freeze better.

SWEETENERS

The following is a list of sweeteners that you might see used in my recipes. It's important to know that the healthiest sweeteners are fresh whole fruits, including fresh dates. That said, dates sometimes compromise texture in recipes. As a chef, I look for great texture, and as a health food advocate, I lean towards fresh dates. But as a consultant helping people embrace a Raw vegan lifestyle, I'm also supportive of helping them transition, which sometimes means using raw agave nectar, or some other easy-to-use sweetener that might not have the healthiest ranking in the Raw food world, but is still much healthier than most sweeteners used in the Standard American Diet.

Most of my recipes can use pitted dates in place of raw agave nectar. There is some debate among Raw food enthusiasts as to whether agave nectar is Raw. The company I use (Madhava®) claims to be Raw and says they do not heat their Raw agave nectar above 118 degrees. If however, you still want to eat the healthiest of sweeteners, then bypass the raw agave nectar and use pitted dates. In most recipes, you can simply substitute 1 - 2 pitted dates for 1 tablespoon of raw agave nectar. Dates won't give you a super creamy texture, but the texture can be improved by making a "date paste" (pureeing pitted and soaked dates – with their soak water, plus some additional water, if necessary – in a food processor fitted with the "S" blade). This, of course, takes a little extra time.

If using raw agave nectar is easier and faster for you, then go ahead and use it; just be sure to buy the Raw version that says they don't heat the agave above 118 degrees (see KristensRaw.com/store for links to this product). And, again, if you're looking to go as far as you can on the spectrum of health, then I recommend using pitted dates. Most of my recipes say raw agave nectar because that is most convenient for people.

Agave Nectar

There are a variety of agave nectars on the market, but again, not all of them are Raw. Make sure it is labeled "Raw" on the bottle *as well as claiming that it isn't processed above 118 degrees*. Just because the label says "Raw" does not necessarily mean it is so... do a double check and make sure it also claims not to be heated above the 118 degrees cut-off. Agave nectar is noteworthy for having a low glycemic index.

Dates

Dates are probably the healthiest of sweeteners, because they're a fresh whole food. Fresh organic dates are filled with nutrition, including calcium and magnesium. I like to call dates, "Nature's Candy."

Feel free to use dates instead of agave or honey in Raw vegan recipes. If a recipe calls for 1/2 cup of raw agave, then you can substitute with approximately 1/2 cup of pitted dates. You can also make your own date sugar by dehydrating pitted dates and then grinding them down. This is a great alternative to Rapadura®.

Honey

Most honey is technically raw, but it is not vegan by most definitions of "vegan" because it is produced by animals, who therefore are at risk of being mistreated. While honey does not have the health risks associated with animal by-products such as eggs or dairy, it can spike the body's natural sugar levels. Agave nectar has a lower, healthier glycemic index and can replace any recipe you find that calls for honey, in a 1 to 1 ratio.

Maple Syrup

Maple syrup is made from boiled sap of the maple tree. It is not considered Raw, but some people still use it as a sweetener in certain dishes.

Rapadura®

This is a dried sugarcane juice, and it's not Raw. It is, however, an unrefined and unbleached organic whole-cane sugar. It imparts a nice deep sweetness to your recipes, even if you only use a little. Feel free to omit it if you'd like to adhere to a strictly Raw program. You can substitute Rapadura with homemade date sugar (see Dates above).

Stevia

This is from the leaf of the stevia plant. It has a sweet taste and doesn't elevate blood sugar levels. It's very sweet, so you'll want to use much less stevia than you would any other sweetener. My mom actually grows her own stevia. It's a great addition in fresh smoothies, for example, to add some sweetness without the calories. You can use the white powdered or liquid version from the store, but these are not Raw. When possible, the best way to have stevia is grow it yourself.

Yacon Syrup

This sweetener has a low glycemic index, making it very attractive to some people. It has a molasses-type flavor that is nice and rich. You can replace raw agave with this sweetener in my recipes, but make sure to get the Raw variety, available at NaturalZing.com. They offer a few different yacon syrups, including one in particular that is not heat-treated. Be sure to choose that one.

SUN-DRIED TOMATOES

By far, the best sun-dried tomatoes are those you make yourself with a dehydrator. If you don't have a dehydrator, make sure you buy the "dry" sun-dried tomatoes, usually found in the bulk section of your health food market. Don't buy the kind that are packed in a jar of oil.

Also... don't buy sun-dried tomatoes if they're really dark (almost black) because these just don't taste as good. Again, I recommend making them yourself if you truly want the freshest flavor possible. It's really fun to do!

EATING WITH YOUR EYES

Most of us, if not all, naturally eat with our eyes before taking a bite of food. So, do yourself a favor and make your eating experience the best ever with the help of a simple, gorgeous presentation. Think of it this way, with real estate, it's always *location, location, location*, right? Well, with food, it's always *presentation, presentation, presentation.*

Luckily, Raw food does this on its own with all of its naturally vibrant and bright colors. But I take it even one step farther – I use my best dishes when I eat. I use my beautiful wine glasses for my smoothies and juices. I use my fancy goblets for many of my desserts. Why? Because I'm worth it. And, so are you! Don't save your good china just for company. Believe me, you'll notice the difference. Eating well is an attitude, and when you take care of yourself, your body will respond in kind.

ONLINE RESOURCES FOR GREAT PRODUCTS

For a complete and detailed list of my favorite kitchen tools, products, and various foods (all available online), please visit: KristensRaw.com/store.

BOOK RECOMMENDATIONS

I highly recommend reading the following life-changing books.

- *Diet for a New America*, by John Robbins
- *The Food Revolution*, by John Robbins
- *The China Study*, by T. Colin Campbell
- *Skinny Bitch*, by Rory Freedman

MEASUREMENT CONVERSIONS

1 tablespoon = 3 teaspoons

1 ounce = 2 tablespoons

1/4 cup = 4 tablespoons

1/3 cup = 5 1/3 tablespoons

1 cup

= 8 ounces

= 16 tablespoons

= 1/2 pint

1/2 quart

= 1 pint

= 2 cups

1 gallon

= 4 quarts

= 8 pints

= 16 cups

= 128 ounces

BASIC RECIPES TO KNOW

Nourishing Rejuvelac

Yield 1 gallon

Rejuvelac is a cheesy-tasting liquid that is rich in enzymes and healthy flora to support a healthy intestine and digestion. Get comfortable making this super easy recipe because its use goes beyond just drinking it between meals.

1 cup soft wheat berries, rye berries, or a mixture
water

Place the wheat berries in a half-gallon jar and fill the jar with water. Screw the lid on the jar and soak the wheat berries overnight(10 - 12 hours) on your counter. The next morning, drain and rinse them. Sprout the wheat berries for 2 days, draining and rinsing 1 - 2 times a day.

Then, fill the jar with purified water and screw on the lid, or cover with cheesecloth secured with a rubber band. Allow to ferment for 24 - 36 hours, or until the desired tartness is achieved. It should have a cheesy, almost tart/lemony flavor and scent.

Strain your rejuvelac into another glass jar and store in the refrigerator for up to 5 - 7 days. For a second batch using the same sprouted wheat berries, fill the same jar of already sprouted berries with water again, and allow to ferment for 24 hours. Strain off the rejuvelac as you did the time before this. You can do this process yet again, noting that each time the rejuvelac gets a little weaker in flavor.

Enjoy 1/4 - 1 cup of *Nourishing Rejuvelac* first thing in the morning and/or between meals. It's best to start with a small amount and work your way up as your body adjusts.

Suggestion:

- For extra nutrition and incredible flavor, *Nourishing Rejuvelac* can be used in various recipes such as Raw vegan cheeses, desserts, smoothies, soups, dressings and more. Simply use it in place of the water required by the recipe.

Crème Fraiche

Yield approximately 2 cups

    1 cup cashews, soaked 1 hour, drained, and rinsed
    1/4 - 1/2 cup *Nourishing Rejuvelac* (see p. 24)
    1 - 2 tablespoons raw agave nectar

Blend the ingredients until smooth. Store in an airtight glass mason jar for up to 5 days. This freezes well, so feel free to make a double batch for future use.

Nut/Seed Milk (regular)

Yield 4 - 5 cups

The creamiest nut/seed milk traditionally comes from hemp seeds, cashews, pine nuts, Brazil nuts or macadamia nuts, although I'm also a huge fan of milks made from walnuts, pecans, hazelnuts, almonds, sesame seeds, and others.

This recipe does not include a sweetener, but when I'm in the mood for a little sweetness, I add a couple of pitted dates or a squirt of raw agave nectar. Yum!

> 1 1/2 cups nuts, soaked 6 - 12 hours, drained and rinsed
>
> 3 1/4 cups water
>
> pinch Himalayan crystal salt, optional

Blend the ingredients until smooth and deliciously creamy. For an even *extra creamy* texture, strain your nut/seed milk through a nut milk bag.

Sweet Nut/Seed Cream (thick)

Yield 2 - 3 cups

> 1 cup nuts or seeds, soaked 6 - 8 hours, drained and rinsed
>
> 1 - 1 1/2 cups water, more if needed
>
> 2 - 3 tablespoons raw agave nectar or 2 - 3 dates, pitted
>
> 1/2 teaspoon vanilla extract, optional

Blend all of the ingredients until smooth.

Raw Mustard

Yield approximately 1 1/2 - 2 cups

> 1 - 2 tablespoons yellow mustard seeds (depending on how "hot" you want it), soaked 1 - 2 hours
>
> 1 1/2 cups extra virgin olive oil or hemp oil
>
> 1 1/2 tablespoons dry mustard powder
>
> 2 tablespoons apple cider vinegar
>
> 2 tablespoons fresh lemon juice
>
> 3 dates, pitted and soaked 30-minutes, drained
>
> 1/2 cup raw agave nectar
>
> 1 teaspoon Himalayan crystal salt
>
> pinch turmeric

Blend all of the ingredients together until smooth. It might be very thick, so if you want, add some water or oil to help thin it out. Adding more oil will help reduce the "heat" if it's too spicy for your taste.

Variation:

- Honey Mustard Version: Add another 1/3 cup raw agave nectar (or more, depending on how sweet you want it)

My Basic Raw Mayonnaise

Yield about 2 1/2 cups

People tell me all the time how much they like this recipe.

1 cup cashews, soaked 1 - 2 hours, drained

1/2 teaspoon paprika

2 cloves garlic

1 teaspoon onion powder

3 tablespoons fresh lemon juice

1/4 cup extra virgin olive oil or hemp oil

2 tablespoons parsley, chopped

2 tablespoons water, if needed

Blend all of the ingredients, except the parsley, until creamy. Pulse in the parsley. *My Basic Raw Mayonnaise* will stay fresh for up to one week in the refrigerator.

CHAPTER 2

THE AMAZING GIFT FROM NATURE

Now widely available in health food stores everywhere, hemp is an amazing plant and superfood that is a powerful addition to everyone's diet, whether you're a child, adult, or senior. To me, hemp is a food that is truly the gift that keeps on giving. If I were stranded on a deserted island and I could only have a few staples with me, I'd choose hemp seeds, coconut water, and a green powder (such as Vitamineral Green).

Hemp foods include hemp seeds, hemp oil, and hemp protein powder. Hemp is high in complete protein with all the essential amino acids as well as essential fatty acids. In short, hemp should be an essential part of everyone's diet.

MANITOBA HARVEST™ HEMP FOODS & OILS – THE BEST!

My favorite brand of hemp seeds and foods is Manitoba Harvest Hemp Foods & Oils. Simply put, they taste the best. The freshness and quality of their hemp products is unsurpassed. They are certified kosher and a USDA certified organic processor. To ensure quality, they grow, process and package all of their own products, giving the highest care and using only the finest hemp seeds. Manitoba Harvest is proud to pay above market price to their farmers, who are shareholders in the company. Furthermore, all of their hemp seeds are original source and contain no Genetically Modified

Organisms (GMOs). They practice sustainable farming and do not spray herbicides or pesticides on the crop. (They also offer USDA certified organic hemp seed for their certified organic products.)

All Manitoba Harvest™ products are tested by a third party laboratory to guarantee quality and freshness and their products contain 0.00% THC so they will not cause a false positive drug test or psychoactive effect. As you can see, Manitoba Harvest Hemp Foods & Oils is the only way to go for your hemp food needs.

HEMP AND ESSENTIAL FATTY ACIDS (EFAs)

There are two essential fatty acids (EFAs) that we must obtain through diet. They are Omega-6 Linoleic Acid (LA) and Omega-3 Linolenic Acid (LNA). Most people don't realize that there is a recommended ratio in how these should be consumed for optimal health. Often, people turn to flax seeds and flax oil to get their essential fatty acids, but flax seeds do not contain the ratio that is recommended by the World Health Organization. Hemp seed oil has the ratio that is closest to the recommended 4:1 (omega-6:omega-3) with a ratio of 3.75:1! Therefore, hemp seed oil can be used ongoing without developing a deficiency or other imbalance of EFAs.

Hemp seed oil is one of the few sources of the super polyunsaturated fatty acid Gamma-Linolenic Acid (GLA). This is an important fat, which can help maintain hormonal balance. The high content of EFAs, along with the high phytosterol content (hemp seeds contain 438mg/100g) found in hemp foods, make them beneficial to cardiovascular health.

HEMP AND AMINO ACIDS

The building blocks of proteins are amino acids. Ten of the twenty amino acids are considered essential because the human body cannot make them, so they must be supplied through your diet. Hemp is a superior choice for protein, and accordingly, amino acids. According to Manitoba Harvest:

> *Many plant proteins are labeled "incomplete" proteins resulting from the low amounts of one or more of the ten essential amino acids. Truth be told, the "incomplete" label is somewhat misleading as all plant proteins do contain each of the essential amino acids. But in most cases (e.g. grains, legumes), levels of one or more amino acid are insufficient for human needs. However, hemp protein supplies enough of each of the essential amino acids to contribute to the human body's requirements.*

One of the most noteworthy aspects of hemp protein is that it is a quality source of certain specific amino acids: arginine and histidine. Both of these are significant for growth during childhood, making hemp an excellent choice of food for children. Hemp also has the sulphur-containing amino acids methionine and cysteine, both of which are needed in the production of vital enzymes.

According to Hemp Line Journal, July - August 1992, pp. 14 - 15, Vol. I No. 1:

> *Hemp is not unique in having all the essential amino acids in its embryonic seed. Flax seeds also contain all the essential amino acids as do many other seeds in the plant kingdom. What is unique about hemp seed*

protein is that 65% of it is globulin edistin. That is the highest in the plant kingdom.

Globulins are one of seven classes of simple proteins. Simple proteins are constructed from amino acids and contain no non-protein substances. Globulins are in seeds and animal blood. Edistins are found in seeds; serum globulin is in blood. Edistins are plant globulins. And globulins along with albumins are classified as globular proteins. All enzymes, antibodies, many hormones, hemoglobin and fibrogin (the body converts fibrogin into non-soluble, fibrin, a blood clotting agent) are globular proteins. They carry out the main work of living.

Albumin, globulin and fibrogin are the three major types of plasma proteins. Plasma is the fluid portion of blood that supplies nutrients to tissues. And the three protein types: serum albumin, serum globulin and fibrogin, compose about 80% of plasma solids. These plasma proteins serve as a reservoir of rapidly available amino acids should any body tissues be in need.

HEMP FOODS

Hemp's value as a food has been known for centuries. Hemp seed oil, for instance, has been a traditional food in China dating back as far as 1500 BC.

Hemp seeds, hemp oil, and hemp protein powder are an important part of my Raw food lifestyle. It's not often that a day goes by that I haven't consumed hemp foods in some form. Hemp is so versatile, delicious, easy to use, and fun.

STORING HEMP

For storage purposes, I recommend freezing your hemp powder, hemp oil, hemp seed butter, and hemp seeds to extend their shelf life and keep them as fresh as possible. Frozen, these foods can be kept for 6 - 12 months, and can therefore be purchased economically in bulk quantities – just freeze what you don't use.

HEMP SEED OIL

Hemp seed oil can be used in smoothies, juices, salad dressings, sauces, dips, desserts and much more. This wonderful oil has a gorgeous fresh green color, exhibiting its notable chlorophyll content. It's extremely decadent, rich and smooth.

As I mentioned earlier, I only use and recommend Manitoba Harvest hemp products... with good reason. There was a time that I couldn't stand hemp oil, because I thought it tasted terrible. I couldn't figure out why this was the case because I loved hemp seeds and hemp protein powder. It turns out, the oil I had wasn't from Manitoba Harvest. The first time I sampled Manitoba's fresh hemp oil, I thought I was in heaven. I was hooked!

Hemp oil is great for your body, internally and externally. I use hemp oil as a makeup remover and all-over hair and body moisturizer. As I stroll around the makeup and beauty product areas at health food stores, one thing is clear... hemp is getting popular with more and more natural beauty product companies.

Note: Even though this is a Raw book, for those of you still cooking, you should not cook with hemp oil because it breaks down and becomes ineffective if exposed to high temperatures.

HEMP SEED NUT (Shelled Hemp Seed)

One of my favorite ways to enjoy hemp is eating the seeds straight out of the bag. Hemp seeds have a lovely texture that is both a little creamy and crunchy with every bite. They're a gorgeous ivory-yellow color tapped with a touch of green. When you use them to make hemp seed butter they blend into a lovely light green color. Hemp seeds are wonderful just snacking on as is. Or, you can add them to soups, salads, cereals, trail mix, yogurt (Raw vegan, of course!), ice cream (Raw vegan, of course), and so much more.

HEMP SEED BUTTER

Ever since I made my first batch of *Raw Hemp Seed Butter* (see recipe, p. 61), it quickly became a staple in my house. I love how its soft texture delicately melts in my mouth. It's the perfect accompaniment to crackers, bread, veggies, fruit, sandwiches, added to smoothies, or just as a spoonful by itself.

HEMP'S PROTEIN POWDER

For those of you looking for more Raw vegan protein in your diet, look no further! The most effective way to get more protein into your diet is with hemp protein powder. It comes full of fiber, all the essential amino acids (in proper proportions!), essential fatty acids, antioxidants, chlorophyll, vitamins and minerals.

Hemp is gaining popularity because it offers an easy to digest source of protein (unlike soy, which is difficult for some people to digest), as well as other important nutrients such as fiber, vitamins, and minerals like magnesium, iron, and phosphorus.

BUT DON'T TAKE MY WORD FOR IT...

Here are some great testimonials from Manitoba Harvest:

"To eat clean and healthy is what works for me, Manitoba Harvest Hemp Foods & Oils fuel my system to work at optimal performance, I 'can' feel the difference. When I first started with Manitoba Harvest Hemp Protein Powder I was surprised to see all the necessary oils and the amount of protein that it contained. I start my day with it and the funny thing is that now I crave it, so it has to be GOOD."

– Otto Flores, professional surfer

"Daily training breaks down my body, hemp foods & oils help rebuild it. Complete protein, Omega 3 & 6 EFAs, and a natural anti-inflammatory, hemp foods & oils supply it all. As an integral part of my training diet hemp foods & oils have allowed me to optimize my performance."

– Brendan Brazier, professional triathlete

"I am just sending a brief message to say how much I enjoy your hemp powder. As a diabetic I find it a great way to add a bit of protein to my morning meal. I only use Manitoba Harvest because it is I think the best."

– Debby Hunter

"I'd heard that hemp seed oil could lower cholesterol so thought I'd see for myself. On March 1, 2005 I bought at bottle of your oil at Wheatsville Co-op here in Austin, TX . I made an appointment with my doctor for March 25th. Then I started taking two tablespoons a day. When I went to the doctor on the 25th, my 'bad' cholestrol had slightly decreased, but my "good" cholestrol had greatly increased.

" I had an unexpected benefit as well. Nine years ago I was diagnosed with fibromyalgia. I also have arthritis in several joints. I had been gradually getting worse, but since I have been taking the hemp oil I am practically pain free and the swelling in my joints has gone down. It's been nothing short of amazing. When my doctor saw my results, he bought some for himself."

– Trish Taylor

"After trying both competitor's hemp protein I can unequivocally say that Manitoba Harvest's Hemp Protein Powder is the best I have tried. It tastes much better and it is quite evident that it is fresher as well. It is obvious that you take great care to ensure a high quality product. Keep doing what your doing, I can see

36

myself using your hemp protein powder in my daily smoothies for years to come."

– Chris Brown

"Climbing is very rigorous and tough on the body. It requires an enormous amount of strength and endurance. This past winter, I began to climb competitively. Although climbing competitions are more like celebrations, or festivals rather than typical competitions, they are extremely difficult and taxing. I started to feel the onset of bursitis/tendonitis in my elbows, a typical climbing injury.

"After a great deal of research, I realized that my diet was lacking in Essential Fatty Acids. Luckily, I found Manitoba Harvest's Hemp Seed Oil. It was the perfect supplement for my diet. The LA:LNA ratio is balanced better than any other plant source, and the fact that the Hemp Seed Oil has GLA makes it a very well rounded source for EFAs.

"Within a week of taking the oil, my symptoms were gone and I felt stronger and had more energy than ever before. I take the Hemp Seed Oil regularly and continue to feel great."

– G. Martizez

GO GREEN WITH HEMP!

Hemp is an extremely important industrial crop that is great for the earth. According to Keith Watson, a hemp crop specialist with Manitoba Agriculture, "Hemp is a sturdy crop

37

that grows tall and fast, which means it out-competes weeds."
Hemp is automatically organic because no pesticides or
herbicides are needed to produce massive yields. This makes it
one of the lowest cost, highest value crops on the planet.

Aside from hemp's amazing food uses, its fiber is just as soft as
cotton, but stronger and much longer-lasting. (Cotton is also
one of the most pesticide-laden crops on the planet, whereas
hemp cultivation requires no pesticides/herbicides and lasts
for years and years.) Hemp oils can be made into biofuel,
biodegradable plastics, and other chemicals (useful for
industries such as automotive manufacturing) that otherwise
must be made from petroleum, the majority of which must be
imported from abroad.

HEMP'S CRAZY & FRUSTRATING LEGAL STATUS

In the U.S., hemp products can be purchased legally. These
can be found in health-food stores, online, and, more and
more every day, in "regular" stores as well, for instance, in
food and clothing products.

But, as of this writing, hemp presently costs much more than it
should, due to rather absurd and backward laws that make it
illegal to grow hemp in the U.S., but legal to import it. This
means that all hemp products sold in the U.S. are necessarily
imported, and cost more accordingly.

According to the Hemp Industries Association, "Hemp
cultivation is among the oldest industries on the planet, dating
back to more than 10,000 years ago when people first began to
make pottery. The *Columbia History of the World* states that

the oldest relic of human industry is a bit of hemp fabric dating back to approximately 8,000 BC."

Hemp played an important part in U.S. history. Columbus' ships – the Nina, Pinta, and Santa Maria – crossed the Pacific with sails made of rugged hemp fabric. George Washington grew hemp on his plantation. Betsy Ross sewed the first American flag out of hemp fabric. The Conestoga wagons that tamed the frontier were covered with hemp canvas. And during World War II, the U.S. government desperately implored U.S. farmers to grow hemp for the war effort, to be used as ropes for the navy. Hemp paper can also be recycled more times than wood-based paper.

But in 1970, growing hemp was outlawed in the U.S. due to... get this... the shape of its leaf! Congress exempted industrial hemp from the Controlled Substances Act, but the newly formed Drug Enforcement Agency ignored this and tagged industrial hemp as a controlled substance. Hemp has no narcotic properties, but it is in the same family as marijuana, with a similar-looking leaf. In the early days of the War on Drugs, federal regulators felt that legal hemp crops would make it difficult to enforce bans on growing marijuana due to possible confusion between the plants. Other Western countries followed suit with similar bans.

After getting slammed by the severe economic impact of several decades of this tragically flawed policy, in the 1990's, nearly all of the other countries reversed their laws banning the growing of hemp, and the crop has flourished abroad ever since, with no negative impact on the enforcement of those nations' drug laws.

The U.S. is the laggard and brunt of jokes now, because we must import one of the world's most valuable, ecologically friendly, and easy-to-grow plants from abroad (mostly from Canada), to the outrage of American farmers and the detriment of consumers' pocketbooks.

Recently, American consumers have begun to become more aware of hemp's advantages, driving growing demand for hemp-based foods and textile products. As this demand has increased, so have import volumes. Several agriculture-intensive U.S. states have challenged the DEA's restrictions in federal court and it is probably just a matter of time before farming hemp is legalized in the U.S. When that happens, you can expect to see both the prices of hemp-related products drop as well as an increase in their availability.

Note: A frustrating and sometimes laughable exchange between states and federal regulators, the battle over hemp's legal status is closely watched by environmentalist and other activist groups. To stay abreast or get involved, visit:

- *Hemp Industries Association (thehia.org)* – A non-profit trade group dedicated to the development of the hemp industry.

- *VoteHemp.com* – This site has a great newsletter and makes it easy to fire off emails to your representatives in Congress. Many politicians are sympathetic to the hemp industry but fear acting on its behalf because the public's confusion about the plant might be used against them by their political opponents.

And finally, buy more hemp! Nothing gets people's attention like the flow of cold, hard cash. The more food and clothing made from hemp you purchase, the faster this amazing plant will be restored to its proper status as the amazing gift from Nature that it is!

CHAPTER 3

DRINKS

CREAMY DREAMY HEMP MILK

Yield 4 cups

When I make a nut or seed milk I usually make it with hemp seeds, because they're packed with delicious nutrition. This is perfect for drinking by itself, adding to smoothies or eating with Raw granola. Yum!

> 2 1/2 cups water, more if desired
>
> 1 1/2 cups hemp seeds
>
> 1 - 2 tablespoons raw agave nectar or 2 - 3 dates, pitted (optional)

Blend all of the ingredients until creamy and smooth. *Creamy Dreamy Hemp Milk* will last up to five days when stored in an airtight container in the refrigerator (mason jars work great).

1-MINUTE HEMP MILK

Yield 1 3/4 cups

This is a super easy way to make hemp milk, and only takes about a minute. Make sure you have *Raw Hemp Seed Butter* on hand (you can make it yourself – see recipe, p. 61 – or buy it from Manitoba Harvest).

1 1/2 - 2 cups water (depending how thick you'd like it)

2 tablespoons *Raw Hemp Seed Butter (see recipe, p. 61)*

1 tablespoon raw agave nectar or 1 date, pitted (optional)

Blend all of the ingredients until smooth and creamy. *1-Minute Hemp Milk* will last up to five days when stored in an airtight container in the refrigerator (mason jars work great).

BODYBUILDER HEMP SHAKE

Yield 1 serving

Whether you love working out or you just want more energy, this drink is the perfect answer!

1 cup water

1 banana, peeled

2 tablespoons hemp protein powder

2 tablespoons goji berries

2 teaspoons raw chocolate powder

1/2 teaspoon mesquite powder*

Blend all of the ingredients together and enjoy this amazing shake that is sure to satisfy anyone.

* Available at NavitasNaturals.com.

CHERRY VANILLA HEMP SHAKE

Yield 2 cups

Cherries are one of my favorite fruits and they taste super delicious in this shake. Cherries are full of some seriously powerful nutrition. This gorgeous dark red fruit is loaded with all kinds of fun "anti" compounds: anti-inflammatory, anti-aging, and anti-cancer.

   1/2 cup water

   1/4 cup hemp seeds

   1 (10oz) bag frozen cherries (or 2 cups fresh cherries, pitted)

   1 teaspoon raw agave nectar or 1 soft date, pitted

   1/2 vanilla bean, chopped

   pinch Himalayan crystal salt

Blend all of the ingredients together until smooth.

CHOCOLATE CARAMEL HEMP SURPRISE

Yield approximately 2 cups

I could drink a cup of this everyday whether it's for breakfast or as a nice little dessert. I love it!

   1 cup water (more if desired)

   3/4 cup hemp seeds

   1 3/4 teaspoons raw carob powder

   (continued)

2 tablespoons raw chocolate powder

1 tablespoon raw agave nectar or 1 - 2 dates, pitted

smidge Himalayan crystal salt

2 handfuls of ice cubes

Blend all of the ingredients until smooth and creamy.

SPICY SUNRISE SMOOTHIE

Yield approximately 5 cups

1 - 2 cups water

3 frozen bananas*

1 stalk celery, chopped

1 large carrot, chopped

1 red Serrano pepper, seeded, destemmed and chopped (or more!)

3 - 5 mint leaves

Blend all of the ingredients until smooth. Enjoy!

* I love using frozen bananas with the spicy Serrano pepper, because it's fun to feel the different experiences play in your mouth (cold bananas, spicy Serrano pepper). Room temperature bananas are fine, but add ice to get the same effect.

HEMP MOCHA LATTE ENGINE STARTER

See photo at KristensRaw.com/photos.

Yield 3 cups

What a beautiful way to start your day!

    2 cups water
    1 cup hemp seeds
    2 soft dates, pitted
    2 tablespoons raw chocolate powder
    2 teaspoons raw agave nectar
    1 teaspoon mesquite powder*
    1 teaspoon coffee extract
    1/4 teaspoon cinnamon
    1/4 teaspoon cayenne
    pinch nutmeg

Blend all of the ingredients together until rich, smooth and creamy. For extra enjoyment, make it warm by blending it longer until you reach the desired temperature (1 - 3 minutes). Enjoy this satiating "coffee fix" any time of the day.

* Available at NavitasNaturals.com.

SUPER POWER HEMP GREEN JUICE

Yield 1 - 2 servings

Looking for some mega nutrition? This juice mixture is power packed with nutrients that are sure to fill you with amazing energy and vitality. For me, I'll drink this all by myself, but feel free to share it with a loved one. ☺

  2 large yellow bell peppers, destemmed
  2 cucumbers
  1/2 bunch parsley
  3 - 5 leaves kale
  2 apples
  1 lime
  1 tablespoon hemp oil
  1 tablespoon green powder (optional)

Juice all of the ingredients except the hemp oil and green powder. Then, whisk in the hemp oil and green powder.

LIVER CLEANING HEMP ELIXIR

Yield 2 - 3 cups

  1 - 2 cups water
  1 apple, cored and chopped
  1 banana, peeled
  1 tablespoon hemp protein powder
  1 tablespoon milk thistle seeds, ground*
  1 teaspoon hemp oil

Blend all of the ingredients together. Enjoy!

* Available at MountainRoseHerbs.com.

GGGRRRR! BEOWULF PROTEIN SMOOTHIE

Yield approximately 2 cups

Here is a powerful, post-workout-fueling, muscle replenishing, rockin' antioxidant filled, blood- circulating smoothie. It's like one-stop-shopping with all of the delicious and nutritious goodies in it!

As I always say... GET HEMPED! Hemp protein is a great addition to everyone's life. It's one of the most effective ways to add a complete protein to your diet with plenty of fiber and omegas (essential fatty acids).

> 1 cup water
> 2 bananas, peeled
> 2 stalks celery, chopped
> 2 soft dates, pitted
> 1/2 teaspoon ginger, peeled and minced
> 1 tablespoon goji berries
> 1 tablespoon hemp protein powder

Blend all of the ingredients until creamy and smooth. Add some ice cubes for a chilly refresher. Enjoy!

BLOOD RED HEMP SUNSET SMOOTHIE

See photo at KristensRaw.com/photos.

Yield 3 cups

This gorgeous smoothie reminds me of the color in the sky when the sun just finishes its set for the evening, and the sky is filled with a beautiful red and orange, so I'm calling it Blood Red Hemp Sunset Smoothie.

> 1 cup water
>
> 3 oranges, peeled
>
> 1 (10oz) bag frozen cherries
>
> 3 tablespoons hemp protein powder
>
> 2 teaspoons raw carob powder
>
> 1/4 - 1/2 teaspoon cayenne

Blend all of the ingredients together. Enjoy!

SUPER SHAKE

Yield approximately 3 cups

> 1 cup water
>
> 1 cup *Creamy Dreamy Hemp Milk*, or more (see recipe, p. 41)
>
> 1 tablespoon chia seeds
>
> 2 tablespoons hemp protein powder
>
> 1 tablespoon raw rice protein powder*
>
> 1 teaspoon green powder**
>
> 1 teaspoon fruits powder***
>
> 1 banana, peeled

Just blend it up, drink it down and feel the power from the essential amino acids, essential fatty acids, vitamins, minerals, and antioxidants go to work for you!

* I like Sun Warrior Protein (visit KristensRaw.com/store for details) because it's both raw and sprouted, which is rare among rice protein powders.

** As of this writing, my favorite brand is Vitamineral Green (visit KristensRaw.com/store for details), but new green powders are always being introduced and I experiment with many of them.

*** This is to add extra antioxidants to your shake. I use Fruits of the Earth powder (visit KristensRaw.com/store for details).

BLISSED-OUT CHOCOLATE RUNNER'S SMOOTHIE

Yield approximately 4 cups

Chia seeds are praised for many things including their fantastic nutrient profile, which proudly boasts iron, boron, essential fatty acids, fiber, and more. Add to that the claims that they may improve heart health, reduce blood pressure, stabilize blood sugar, help people lose weight from giving them extra stamina, energy, and curbing hunger, and you might become a fan of these little guys, too. They're superstars in my book.

    1 - 2 cups water
    2 bananas, peeled
    1 1/2 cups blueberries
    1 1/2 cups spinach
    3 tablespoons chia seeds

    (continued)

2 tablespoons hemp protein powder

2 tablespoons raw chocolate powder

1/2 teaspoon cinnamon

1 - 2 cups ice, optional

Blend all of the ingredients until smooth and enjoy.

SMILING SMOOTHIE

Yield 4 cups

When I make this smoothie, I smile from ear to ear with every swig of it.

Did you know that bananas are known to help fight bloating as a result of the potassium content in them? Ladies, if any of you are experiencing excess bloat from PMS, then bring on the bananas (and this smoothie does just that).

1 cup water

3 frozen bananas, peeled

2 oranges, peeled and seeded

1/2 cup dried coconut, shredded & unsweetened

2 tablespoons raw chocolate powder

2 tablespoons hemp protein powder

1 teaspoon vanilla extract

Blend all of the ingredients thoroughly and smile with every swig.

HEMP DICHOTOMY COCKTAIL

Yield 1 1/2 cups

Here is a relaxing, yet stimulating, beverage. I can't imagine a better way to have these two favorites of mine together... wine and chocolate. Such an elegant love affair.

Oh, and by the way, cloves are an excellent mouth freshener... perfect if you're sharing this cocktail with a loved one.

> 3/4 cup organic, vegan red wine
>
> 2 cloves, crushed
>
> 1/2 cup *Creamy Dreamy Hemp Milk* (see recipe, p. 41)
>
> 1 teaspoon raw dark (or blue) agave nectar*
>
> 1 teaspoon raw chocolate powder

Blend all of the ingredients in a blender until smooth and serve in a sexy wine glass.

* I prefer Wholesome Sweetner's Organic Raw Blue Agave.

CHAPTER 4

QUICKIE SNACKS

HEMP BANANA SMASH

Yield 1 - 2 servings

This is a great snack or breakfast for the whole family to enjoy. And super fast. In fact, it's really fun for kids to make!

    2 bananas, peeled and chopped
    2 tablespoons goji berries
    2 teaspoons hemp seeds
    1 teaspoon raw cacao nibs, optional
    1 teaspoon hemp protein powder
    1/2 teaspoon chia seeds

Smash up the banana, goji berries, hemp seeds, cacao nibs, hemp powder and chia seeds together until it resembles a chunky pudding.

This is a great recipe to play with and have fun by adding other wonderful flavors such as raw chocolate powder, diced dried apricots or dried cherries, cinnamon, nutmeg, cayenne pepper, green powder (I usually use Vitamineral Green Powder), a squeeze of fresh lemon, lime or orange juice. There are so many wonderful alternatives to this basic recipe that you and your family will never get bored with it.

GOOD OL' HEMP SEEDS-N-RAISINS

Yield 1 1/2 cups

This is one of my favorite snacks ever (and perfect for munching on when going to the movies)! I keep a small bag of this with me everywhere I go.

> 1 cup hemp seeds
> 1/2 cup raisins

Place the hemp seeds and raisins in a glass mason jar and shake to mix them up. Yum!

Variation:

- Sometimes I like to add 1/4 teaspoon cinnamon for a little extra flare and fun. Experiment with other flavors... the possibilities are endless (imagine these variations: fennel powder or seeds, nutmeg, cayenne pepper, dried basil, Chinese 5-spice, etc)

HEMP BANANAS

Yield 1 serving

This is a great snack or breakfast for children (and you!).

> 1 banana, peeled
> 1 - 2 tablespoons hemp seeds

Roll the banana in the hemp seeds and enjoy this super nutritious snack.

If you're on the run, simply take the banana with you (unpeeled) and a little baggie of hemp seeds. When you're ready to eat it, just peel the banana and dip it into the bag of hemp seeds bite by bite. Yum! Sometimes, the simplest things in life are the best.

POWER PACKED HEMP TRAIL MIX

Yield approximately 1 3/4 cups

I love munching on this when I'm on a long hike. It's the perfect snack while on the trail.

    1 cup hemp seeds
    1/3 cup currants
    1/3 cup goji berries
    1/4 cup raw cacao nibs

Place all of the ingredients in a glass mason jar and shake to mix them up. Take some in a little baggie on your next hike.

MAGIC APPLESAUCE

Yield approximately 2 cups

I call this magic applesauce for a few reasons: 1) It's full of nutrition, 2) It's sweet and super delicious, 3) It's perfect for kids any time of the day, what kids don't like "magic" food (myself included!), and 4) it's so EASY!

2 apples, cored and chopped

1 banana, peeled

2 tablespoons ground flax seed

2 tablespoons golden raisins

2 tablespoons raw agave nectar

1 tablespoon hemp protein powder

1 tablespoon raw carob powder

1/4 teaspoon cinnamon

Using a food processor, fitted with the "S" blade, process all of the ingredients until you reach your desired texture (smooth or with some little chunks). Enjoy immediately after making.

CHAPTER 5

BREAD & CRACKERS

SOFT-N-SAVORY HEMP ONION BREAD

See photo at KristensRaw.com/photos.

Yield approximately 32 pieces

Every time you come to my house, you'll find this in the refrigerator. It's perfect for snacking on by itself, dipped in Raw hummus, or spread with *Raw Hemp Seed Butter* (see recipe, p. 61).

> 3/4 cup hemp seeds (lightly ground)
> 3/4 cup chia seeds
> 3 pounds red onions, chopped
> 2 medium tomatoes, chopped
> 1 cup spinach, packed
> 1/3 cup raw agave nectar
> 1/3 cup tamari, wheat-free
> 1/4 cup hemp protein powder

Place the ground hemp seeds and whole chia seeds in a large bowl and set aside. Process the onions, tomatoes and spinach in a food processor, fitted with the "S" blade, into small pieces (don't let it get too mushy though).

Add the onion mixture and the remaining ingredients to the bowl of seeds and stir well to mix. Let the batter sit for 5 minutes. If you find that the batter is too "wet" then add more chia seeds to soak it up (1 - 2 tablespoons at a time and wait a few minutes).

Use approximately 4 cups per tray and spread the batter onto 2 dehydrator trays, each lined with a Paraflexx sheet. Dehydrate at 130 - 140 degrees for one hour. Lower the temperature to 105 degrees and dehydrate another 8 hours.

Flip the bread over onto another dehydrator tray and peel off the Paraflexx sheet. Dehydrate another 6 - 10 hours (until you reach your desired dryness – I like mine a little moist). Cut into 16 squares per tray. These are best stored in the refrigerator.

EASY HEMP CRACKERS

Yield 20 crackers

These are easy and delish! No soaking or "pre" steps required. Make a few batches and have them on hand for snacking!

    1 cup chia seeds (or flax seeds)
    1/4 cup hemp oil
    1 cup water
    1/4 cup fresh basil, packed
    1 1/2 tablespoons fresh rosemary
    1 teaspoon onion powder
    Juice from 1 lime
    1/2 teaspoon Himalayan crystal salt

Use your dry blender or coffee grinder to grind the chia seeds into a meal. Transfer them to a large bowl. Blend the remaining ingredients until smooth.

Pour the blended mixture into the bowl with the chia meal and stir by hand quickly to mix. Immediately spread the batter (using an offset spatula and/or your hands) onto a dehydrator tray lined with a Paraflexx sheet.

Score them to the desired size (I score about 20 medium sized crackers). Dehydrate at 130 - 140 degrees for one hour. Flip onto another dehydrator tray and peel off the Paraflexx sheet. At this point you might be able to break them apart by the scored lines you made. Continue dehydrating at 105 degrees until dry (6 - 10 hours).

Serving suggestions:

- Dip these into Raw soups, purees, or pates
- Spread into rounds before dehydrating and make delicious, perfect pizza crusts

CHAPTER 6

SEED BUTTER, SPREADS, DIP & SAUCE

RAW HEMP SEED BUTTER

Yield 1 cup

This creamy and nutritious *Raw Hemp Seed Butter* is perfect for using in a quick batch of *1-Minute Hemp Milk* (see recipe, p. 41) or for spreading onto crackers and slices of fruit.

I make this once a month so I always have it on hand. I recommend making a double or triple batch and freezing it in separate containers. It tastes a lot like peanut butter and it's so easy!

> 2 cups hemp seeds
> pinch Himalayan crystal salt

Place the hemp seeds and the salt in a food processor, fitted with the "S" blade. Process until smooth and creamy (about 4 - 5 minutes), stopping and scraping down the sides every couple of minutes. *Raw Hemp Seed Butter* will last up to a month in your refrigerator when stored in an airtight container (glass mason jars are perfect). This also freezes wonderfully.

MISO HEMP CHEESE SPREAD

Yield approximately 1 1/2 cups

Ooh... this is a fabulous cheese spread. I love dipping carrot and celery sticks into it. So delicious!

    1 cup hemp seeds
    1/2 cup water, more as needed
    2 - 3 cloves garlic
    1 tablespoon *Garlic Red Pepper Miso**
    1 tablespoon light miso
    2 tablespoons fresh lime or lemon juice
    1 tablespoon coconut oil
    1 teaspoon fresh grated lemon zest
    1/4 teaspoon black pepper

Blend all of the ingredients until creamy, adding a little more water as needed to blend it thoroughly. *Miso Hemp Cheese Spread* will last up to 5-days when stored in an airtight container in your refrigerator. This freezes well, too.

* Garlic Red Pepper Miso is available from my favorite source of miso, South River Miso (SouthRiverMiso.com) and it's soy-free, too!

ASIAN HEMP CHEESE SPREAD

Yield 1 1/4 cups

Simple, easy and seriously nutritious cheese spread. Enjoy on crackers, bread, fruit, and vegetables.

1 cup hemp seeds

1/3 cup water, more as needed

2 cloves garlic

2 tablespoons tamari, wheat-free

3 tablespoons fresh lemon juice

2 tablespoons coconut oil

1 tablespoon fresh ginger, grated

1/4 teaspoon ginger powder

Blend all of the ingredients until creamy, adding a little more water as needed to blend it thoroughly. *Asian Hemp Cheese Spread* will last up to 5-days when stored in an airtight container in your refrigerator. This freezes well, too.

RAW HEMP ZA'ATAR

See photo at KristensRaw.com/photos (sprinkled on Hemp Hummus Dip).

Yield 1/4 cup

Za'atar is a mixture of spices hailing from the Middle East. It's usually made with toasted sesame seeds, but I'm making it Raw hemp style.

In Lebanon, there is a belief that this spice mixture makes a strong body and alert mind. In certain areas of the world, children are encouraged to eat za'atar in some fashion for breakfast before an exam (sprinkled on a Raw hummus sandwich is perfect).

2 tablespoons sumac*

1 tablespoon dried thyme

1 tablespoon dried oregano

1 tablespoon dried marjoram

2 teaspoons hemp seeds

1/2 teaspoon Himalayan crystal salt

Combine all of the ingredients in a glass mason jar and shake to mix. I love sprinkling this on top of *Hemp Hummus Dip* (see recipe below), sprinkled on top of salads or mixed with hemp oil and used as a dip for veggies and Raw bread or crackers (see *Hemp Oil Za'atar Dressing & Dip*, p. 67).

* Available at most Middle Eastern stores.

HEMP HUMMUS DIP

See photo at KristensRaw.com/photos.

Yield 2 cups

2 cups zucchini, peeled and chopped (approximately 2 medium zucchini)

1/4 cup fresh lemon juice

1/4 cup raw tahini

1/2 cup *Raw Hemp Seed Butter* (see recipe, p. 61)

2 cloves garlic

2 teaspoons cumin

1 teaspoon Himalayan crystal salt

Blend all of the ingredients until creamy. Serve with Raw breads, crackers, sliced vegetables or chopped fruit. For more spunk, add a tablespoon of *Raw Hemp Za'atar* (see recipe, p. 63).

CHEEZY HEMP NACHO SAUCE

Yield approximately 1 1/2 cups

This is so delicious – trust me! It's perfect anytime, including showing off at the next party you host or attend. Every time I make it, my husband licks the bowl. ☺

 1/3 cup water

 1 clove garlic

 2 tablespoons fresh lemon juice

 1 red bell pepper, seeded, rough chopped (approximately 1 cup)

 1 cup hemp seeds

 2 1/2 tablespoons nutritional yeast flakes

 1 tablespoon chili powder

 2 teaspoons tamari, wheat-free

 1/2 teaspoon Himalayan crystal salt

 1/2 teaspoon garlic powder

 1/4 teaspoon cayenne pepper

 1/8 teaspoon turmeric powder

Blend all of the ingredients in a blender until smooth and creamy. This can be stored in the refrigerator for up to four days.

Serving suggestions:

- Use this as a sauce for dipping fresh veggies or corn chips
- This also makes a delicious dressing on a hearty salad with romaine lettuce and chopped tomatoes

CINNAMON DELIGHT HEMP SPREAD

Yield 1/2 cup

This is an easy, delicious and nutritious spread for you and your family (especially kids!). I love serving it with sliced apples. Yum!

1/2 cup *Raw Hemp Seed Butter* (see recipe, p. 61)

2 teaspoons raw agave nectar

1/2 teaspoon cinnamon

pinch nutmeg

pinch Himalayan crystal salt

Stir all of the ingredients together in a bowl, or if necessary, use a food processor, fitted with the "S" blade.

CHAPTER 7

POWER SALADS & DRESSINGS

HEMP OIL ZA'ATAR DRESSING & DIP

Yield 1 cup

> 1 cup hemp oil
>
> 1 1/2 tablespoons *Raw Hemp Za'atar* (see recipe p. 63)

Shake both the oil and *Raw Hemp Za'atar* together in a covered glass mason jar.

Serving suggestions:

- Pour 1/4 cup onto a shallow plate and use for dipping bread
- Use 2 tablespoons of this (along with 1 - 2 tablespoons fresh lemon juice and a pinch of Himalayan crystal salt) as a divine dressing over any green salad
- Serve 3 - 4 tablespoons of this with a squeeze of fresh citrus over spiralized zucchini noodles or other chopped vegetables for a wonderful meal

FENNEL KALE ORANGE HEMP SALAD

See photo at KristensRaw.com/photos.

Yield 2 - 3 servings

This highly nutritious salad is refreshing, delicious, and full of flavors that combine effortlessly to deliver one awesome salad.

Kale freakin' rocks the nutrient house! And, no, it's not something that is just meant to decorate salad bars (as my husband used to think – ha ha!). It's loaded with antioxidants and phytonutrients shown to help fight cancer, aid in detoxification, and fill you up with super star nutrition including iron, calcium, protein, fiber, vitamins A, C, K and much more!

1 small - medium bunch curly kale

2 tablespoons fresh lemon juice

2 tablespoons hemp oil

3/4 teaspoon fresh orange zest

1/4 teaspoon Himalayan crystal salt

pinch nutmeg

1 cup fennel bulb, thinly sliced*

1 cup orange, peeled, seeded & chopped

8 kalamata olives, pitted & chopped

1 tablespoon hemp seeds

1 tablespoon fennel leaves, chopped

Destem the kale. You can leave the more tender parts of the stem (toward the top of each leaf) in the salad, but the harder stems toward the bottom of each leaf should be torn out. Tear apart the kale leaves (or use a knife and chop them) into bite-size pieces.

Place the torn kale into a large bowl. Add the lemon juice, hemp oil, orange zest, salt, and nutmeg. Take a minute and massage all of these ingredients together with your hands. Add the fennel, orange, olives, hemp seeds, and fennel leaves, and gently toss to mix. Enjoy!

* I use a handheld V-slicer. Visit KristensRaw.com/store for details.

MIGHTY TABOULI HEMP SALAD

Yield 3 - 4 servings

This addictive salad is full of powerful nutrition. Did you know that both cilantro and parsley aid in detoxification and play a significant role in anti-aging?

The Salad

1 bunch fresh parsley

1 bunch fresh cilantro

1/2 bunch green onions, chopped

2 tablespoons fresh mint, minced

2 carrots, diced

1 red bell pepper, destemmed, seeded and diced

2 Roma tomatoes, chopped

1 avocado, pitted, peeled, and diced

1/3 cup hemp seeds

3 tablespoons golden raisins

The Dressing

2 tablespoons hemp oil

2 tablespoons fresh lemon juice

2 teaspoons raw agave nectar

1/2 teaspoon Himalayan crystal salt

dash cinnamon

dash nutmeg

dash black pepper

Place the parsley, cilantro, green onions, and mint in a food processor, fitted with the "S" blade, and pulse until chopped. Transfer to a large bowl. Add the carrots, bell pepper, tomatoes, avocado, hemp seeds and golden raisins to the parsley mixture and toss to combine.

In a small bowl, whisk together the dressing ingredients. Pour this over the salad, gently toss, and enjoy this refreshing and highly nutritious salad.

HEMP OMEGA CAESAR DRESSING

Yield 2 cups

For anyone looking to have a delicious Raw vegan Caesar dressing, then look no more! You'll be amazed that this dressing is made from plants.

1 cup water

1/2 cup hemp oil or olive oil

(continued)

1/4 cup fresh lemon juice

1/2 cup hemp seeds

2 cloves garlic

1 tablespoon raw agave nectar

1 tablespoon dulse

3/4 teaspoon mustard seeds

1/2 teaspoon Himalayan crystal salt

zest of 1/2 lemon

Blend all of the ingredients until creamy, and enjoy over a salad of fresh, crisp Romaine lettuce.

"IT'S PARTY TIME" HEMP SALAD

Yield approximately 3 quarts (10 - 14 cups)

If you're not eating enough cabbage, now is your chance to get more into your diet and *love it*. Cabbage is loaded with nutritional benefits and cancer-fighting ability because of its phytonutrient profile. But cabbage's awesome resume doesn't stop there... it offers you vitamins C, K, B6, calcium, magnesium, potassium, beta-carotene, manganese, fiber, folate, and omega 3 fatty acids.

This amazing salad is gorgeous, crunchy, chewy, savory and sweet all in one. It's a true party in your mouth when eating this brilliant salad. I'm known to make a batch of this and eat it for days in a row. Yum!

The Salad Mixture

1 large fennel bulb, shredded

4 carrots, shredded

1 head purple cabbage, shredded

3/4 heaping cup currants

1/3 cup hemp seeds

The Dressing

1 cup hemp oil

2 tablespoons fresh lime juice

2 tablespoons water

1 tablespoon apple cider vinegar

1 tablespoon chili powder

1 teaspoon raw agave nectar

1/2 teaspoon powdered mustard

1 clove garlic

1/2 teaspoon cumin

1/2 teaspoon Himalayan crystal salt

1/2 teaspoon black pepper

1/8 teaspoon cayenne pepper

Place the salad ingredients in a large bowl and gently toss. Blend all of the dressing ingredients together, and pour over the salad mixture. Toss well. Enjoy!

Serving suggestion:

- This makes a lot of salad, which makes it perfect for a party, or for a busy person who doesn't mind eating the same thing a few days in a row as leftovers. Otherwise, you can easily cut the recipe in half.

HEMP GREEK OLIVE DRESSING

Yield 1 1/4 cups

    1/2 cup water
    1/2 cup hemp oil
    1/4 cup fresh lime juice
    2 teaspoons raw agave nectar
    2 cloves garlic
    1/2 teaspoon dried rosemary
    1/4 teaspoon Himalayan crystal salt
    1/4 cup fresh basil
    1/2 cup Greek olives, pitted

Blend all of the ingredients together, except the basil and olives, until creamy. Add the basil and pulse to chop. Add the pitted olives and pulse to chop, but don't over blend. You want the dressing to have texture from the minced olives. Serve over a fresh green salad with chopped tomatoes, zucchini, and carrots.

SPICED HEMP PINEAPPLE DRESSING

Yield 1 1/2 cups

This is a great dressing with a little kick!

1/4 cup dried pineapple, soaked 15 minutes, drained and chopped

1 cup water

1/2 cup hemp seeds

1 clove garlic

3 tablespoons fresh lemon juice

1 tablespoon Italian seasoning

1 teaspoon raw agave nectar or 1 soft date, pitted

3/4 teaspoon Himalayan crystal salt

1/4 teaspoon cayenne pepper (or more to taste)

Blend all of the ingredients until smooth.

ZESTY CILANTRO LIME DRESSING

Yield 1 cup

The ingredients in this recipe come together flawlessly.

1/4 cup water

1/4 cup hemp oil

1/4 cup olive oil

1/4 cup fresh lime juice

1/3 cup cilantro, packed

2 soft dates, pitted

1/2 teaspoon fresh lime zest

1/2 teaspoon onion powder

1/4 - 1/2 teaspoon chili powder

1/4 teaspoon Himalayan crystal salt

Blend all of the ingredients until smooth and enjoy on top of your favorite leafy greens and vegetables.

EXQUISITE HEMP OIL DRESSING

Yield 1 cup

This dressing is EASY and fabulous. I'm always getting compliments on it.

> 1/3 cup water
> 1/2 cup hemp seed oil
> Juice of 1 lemon
> 1 heaping tablespoon *Garlic Red Pepper Miso**
> 1 clove garlic
> 1/2 teaspoon powdered mustard

Blend the ingredients until creamy and enjoy on your next salad.

* This dressing would be great with any miso, but I'm particularly fond of making it with South River's (soy free) Garlic Red Pepper Miso available at SouthRiverMiso.com.

HEMP MUSTARD SEED DRESSING

Yield 1 cup

D-E-L-I-C-I-O-U-S!!!!

1/3 cup water

1/2 cup hemp oil

2 tablespoons fresh lemon juice

1 teaspoon onion powder

1 clove garlic

2 tablespoons fresh dill

1 tablespoon raw agave nectar or 1 - 2 soft dates, pitted

1/2 - 1 teaspoon mustard seeds (depending on how spicy you like it!)

1/2 teaspoon Himalayan crystal salt

Blend all of the ingredients together and enjoy!

MISO HEMP BUTTER DRESSING

Yield 1 1/2 cups

A wonderful, unique dressing that is loaded with flavor. It's one of my mom's favorites.

1/2 cup water

1/2 cup *Raw Hemp Seed Butter* (*see recipe, p. 61*)

1/2 inch fresh ginger, chopped (more or less, as desired)

1 clove garlic

2 tablespoons light miso

2 tablespoons fresh lemon juice

1 tablespoon tamari, wheat-free

1/2 teaspoon cumin powder

1/8 teaspoon cayenne pepper

Blend all of the ingredients together until smooth.

KING GARLIC HEMP DRESSING

Yield 1 1/2 cups

I use the word "King" before "Garlic" because in my mind, garlic is indeed the king of seasoning. (Ginger is the queen.) Garlic is loaded with antioxidants, and it's one of the world's oldest medicinal foods.

Back in the old, old days, garlic was given to soldiers to keep them healthy and fight infection, as well as to Egyptian slaves building the pyramids to give them stamina. It's also been said that it helps ward off vampires!

  1 cup hemp oil
  1/2 cup fresh lemon juice
  3 large cloves garlic
  1 1/2 teaspoons Italian seasoning
  1/2 teaspoon Himalayan crystal salt

Blend all of the ingredients thoroughly (I let my high speed blender run 30 - 45ish seconds).

CHAPTER 8

SOUPS

SPINACH THYME SOUP – *AWARD WINNING*

See photo at KristensRaw.com/photos.

Yield 4 servings

This recipe won an award in a contest featured in VegNews magazine. It is a favorite among clients, family and friends.

 5 cups spinach

 1 cup water

 3/4 cup fresh orange juice

 1 1/2 cups zucchini, chopped

 1/2 cup hemp oil

 1 clove garlic

 2 tablespoons *Garlic Red Pepper Miso**

 1 tablespoon apple cider vinegar

 1 tablespoon raw agave nectar

 1 1/2 tablespoons dried basil

 1 1/2 tablespoons dried thyme

 2 teaspoons onion powder

 1/4 teaspoon Himalayan crystal salt

 1/4 teaspoon nutmeg

 1/8 teaspoon cayenne pepper

Blend everything together until creamy. For extra pizazz, serve this delicious soup garnished with sprouts.

* This is my favorite brand of miso. It's so delicious and they offer some soy-free varieties, including the one used in this recipe. For more information, check out SouthRiverMiso.com.

SAVORY CARROT HEMP SOUP

Yield approximately 4 cups

This soup is simply exquisite with delicious and nutritious carrot juice, hemp seeds, zucchini and more.

> 2 cups fresh carrot juice
> 1/2 cup water
> 1/2 cup hemp seeds
> 1/2 cup cashews (unsoaked)
> 1 zucchini, peeled and chopped
> 3 tablespoons fresh lime juice
> 1 clove garlic
> 1 1/2 teaspoons Himalayan crystal salt
> 1 teaspoon cumin
> 1 teaspoon garlic powder
> 1/8 teaspoon cayenne pepper
> dash cinnamon

Blend all of the ingredients until smooth.

Serving suggestion:

- Garnish using 1/4 cup hemp seeds (1 tablespoon per 1 cup serving)

VAMPY HEMP SOUP

See photo on cover and at KristensRaw.com/photos.

Yield 5 cups

The color alone is worth making this soup. This is a sure way to impress your friends and loved ones... with a vibrantly succulent and sassy soup.

    1 cup water

    1 lb tomatoes, chopped (approximately 2 - 3 tomatoes)

    1 cup beet, chopped

    1/4 cup hemp seeds

    1/4 cup hemp oil

    1 tablespoon raw agave nectar (or 1 - 2 soft dates, pitted)

    1/2 cup fresh orange juice

    1 teaspoon onion powder

    1 teaspoon Himalayan crystal salt

    1/4 teaspoon white pepper

    1/4 - 1/2 teaspoon cayenne pepper

Blend all of the ingredients until smooth and thoroughly blended (approximately 1 - 2 minutes). Garnish with fresh green sprouts. Enjoy!

ITALIAN STALLION HEMP BISQUE

Yield 2 cups

Mama Mia! This recipe is creamy, inviting, and full of flavor. I love making a triple batch of it and having it as part of my lunch and dinner for three days in a row!

- 1 cup water
- 1/2 cup hemp seeds
- 1 cup zucchini, chopped
- 1/4 cup fresh basil, packed
- 1 clove garlic
- 2 soft dates, pitted
- 2 tablespoons fresh lemon juice
- 1 tablespoon fresh oregano
- 1 tablespoon sun-dried tomato powder*
- 1/2 teaspoon Himalayan crystal salt
- pinch cinnamon

Blend all of the ingredients until creamy.

* To make sun-dried tomato powder, grind sun-dried tomatoes in a dry blender or coffee grinder.

CHAPTER 9

LUNCH & DINNER

DECADENT CILANTRO GINGER HEMP PESTO

Yield approximately 1 cup

This fabulous variation of traditional pesto is sweetly delicious. It's very filling, so while you might think you're eating this as a side dish, it can serve as a meal, too! YUM!

- 2 bunches cilantro
- 1/2 cup hemp seeds
- 2 tablespoons raw agave nectar
- 2 tablespoons fresh grated ginger
- 1/2 teaspoon Himalayan crystal salt
- 1/8 teaspoon cayenne pepper
- 1/2 cup coconut oil
- 2 - 3 carrots, shredded (more if desired)

Process all of the ingredients, except the oil and carrots, in a food processor, fitted with the "S" blade. While the processor is still running, slowly add the oil. Serve the pesto on top of the shredded carrots.

When you make this ahead of time and store it in the refrigerator, the coconut oil will solidify; therefore, be sure to let it sit at room temperature for a short while to soften before serving.

Serving suggestions:

- This is great with any vegetable crudités
- Serve on top of spiralized red and/or golden beets or zucchini

ROSEMARY HEMP VEGETABLE BLEND

Yield 4 cups

This is a great dish to serve as a side dish or an entire meal. It's also perfect for serving alongside a cooked vegan meal (when you're trying to sneak some Raw food into other people's diets).

The Vegetable Blend

1 cup red bell pepper, diced

1 cup fennel bulb, diced

1 cup zucchini, diced

1 cup carrots, diced

1/4 cup hemp seeds

The Marinade/Sauce

    1 clove garlic

    3 tablespoons hemp oil

    2 tablespoons fresh lemon juice

    1 tablespoon fresh rosemary, lightly minced

    1 tablespoon tamari, wheat-free

    1/4 teaspoon Himalayan crystal salt

    1/4 teaspoon onion powder

    1/8 teaspoon cayenne pepper

Place the chopped vegetables and hemp seeds in to a glass baking dish and toss to mix.

Blend or whisk all of the marinade/sauce ingredients together. Pour the marinade/sauce ingredients over the vegetable blend and toss to ensure all the vegetables get covered. At this point you can eat the delicious vegetable blend, or you can marinate it (covered) in your refrigerator for a day, or you can place the mixture in your dehydrator (my favorite option) at 130 - 140 degrees for 45 minutes. Lower the temperature to 105 degrees and continue dehydrating until it's warm.

CHINESE HEMP NOODLES – *AWARD WINNING*

See photo at KristensRaw.com/photos.

Yield 4 servings

This popular recipe won an award in a contest featured in VegNews magazine.

With noodles originally coming from China, I wanted to create a recipe with oriental flavors and noodles. This recipe has turned out to be one of our favorites at home. And, it's great to take to family and friend get-togethers as your dish to pass.

The Sauce

3 tablespoons water

3 tablespoons hemp oil

2 tablespoons organic, vegan red wine (or more!)

2 tablespoons miso

2 tablespoons raw agave nectar

1 tablespoon fresh ginger, grated

2 teaspoons tamari, wheat-free

1/4 cup hemp seeds

The Noodles Blend

4 - 5 zucchini, peeled and spiralized into noodles*

1 - 2 red bell peppers, destemmed, seeded and minced

Place the noodles and the minced bell pepper(s) in a large bowl and toss. Blend all of the sauce ingredients together, except for the hemp seeds. Pour the sauce into a glass mason jar and stir in the hemp seeds. Just before serving, pour about 1/2 cup of the sauce over the noodles blend and toss to mix. Add more sauce if desired. Store any left over sauce in a glass mason jar.

* If you don't have a spiralizer or turning slicer, then use a vegetable peeler and make fettuccini-style noodles.

Variations:

- Add 1/2 cup chopped cilantro or parsley to the noodles blend
- This sauce is scrumptious served as a dressing over chopped Swiss chard and cucumbers

CARROT DISCS WITH CURRY HEMP SAUCE

Yield 1 cup sauce (4 - 5 small servings)

This creamy sauce with crunchy carrot discs is wonderful. Sometimes I eat this as a side dish with my main meal or I eat it as a main salad and have two meals out of it.

    1/2 cup water
    1/2 cup hemp seeds
    1 tablespoon curry
    1 teaspoon onion powder
    2 teaspoons fresh ginger, grated
    1 1/2 teaspoons raw agave nectar or 1 soft date, pitted
    1 teaspoon garlic, chopped
    1/4 teaspoon Himalayan crystal salt
    dash black pepper
    juice of 1/2 lemon
    1/4 cup cilantro
    1/4 cup currants
    4 - 5 cups carrot discs (4 - 5 medium carrots)

Blend all of the ingredients, except for the cilantro, currants and carrot discs, until creamy. Pulse in the cilantro briefly.

Transfer the sauce to a bowl and stir in the currants. Set aside the sauce.

Using a mandoline, slice the carrots into discs. If you don't have a mandoline, you can spiralize the carrots using a spiralizer or you can simply dice the carrots.

Serve 1 cup of carrots with 2 - 3 tablespoons of sauce.

SAVORY PROTEIN STUFFED MUSHROOMS

Yield 16 - 20 stuffed mushrooms

Everyone loves this recipe, especially non-Raw fooders... they can't believe it's actually Raw. I usually make the recipe as stuffed mushrooms, but the stuffing is also delicious in red bell peppers or zucchini boats.

The Mushrooms & the Marinade

16 - 20 mushrooms

1/4 cup hemp oil or olive oil

1 tablespoon tamari, wheat-free

1 tablespoon fresh lime juice

The Stuffing

3/4 cup hemp seeds

3/4 cup zucchini, chopped

(continued)

1/2 cup carrot, chopped

1/2 cup parsley or cilantro, packed

1 large clove garlic, chopped

1/2 teaspoon cumin

Juice of 1/2 lime

2 teaspoons tamari, wheat-free

For the Marinade

Wipe the mushrooms clean by using a damp paper towel or dishtowel. Put the marinade ingredients in a glass baking dish and briefly whisk together.

Cut a light "X" in the top surface of each mushroom and place the mushrooms "X" side down in the glass baking dish so the marinade is absorbed into the "X." Let them set in the marinade while you make the stuffing.

For the Stuffing

Place all of the ingredients in a food processor, fitted with the "S" blade, and process until semi-smooth. It's nice not to process completely or the colors blend too much. Use 1 - 2 teaspoons and stuff each mushroom. Enjoy!

To make these mushrooms extra delicious, place them in your dehydrator at 135 degrees for 45 minutes and enjoy them slightly warmed.

Store any leftover stuffing in an airtight container in the refrigerator for up to four days. You can store leftover stuffed mushrooms in an airtight container in the refrigerator for two days (reheat in your dehydrator if desired).

Serving suggestions:

- Make a terrific sandwich by spreading the stuffing on a leaf of Swiss chard (or a collard green) and rolling it into a sandwich (add some chopped olives, herbs and a drizzle of hemp oil)
- Try this recipe stuffed in red bell peppers or zucchini boats (cut zucchini in half and seed it, then fill it with the stuffing)

SPICY-N-SWEET FITNESS NOODLES

Yield 1 1/2 cups sauce, approximately 4 - 6 servings

This is one of my favorite recipes by far! I make mine EXTRA HOT to get that endorphin feel-good rush, boost my metabolism, and make me want to get up and get FIT!

The Sauce

2/3 cup water

1/2 cup *Raw Hemp Seed Butter* (see recipe, p. 61)

1 - 2 red Serrano peppers, destemmed and seeded (or use habanero pepper(s) – *How **HOT** can you go???*)

1 clove garlic

1 tablespoon raw agave nectar

2 teaspoons apple cider vinegar

1/2 teaspoon onion powder

1/4 teaspoon Himalayan crystal salt

1/4 teaspoon paprika

(continued)

1/4 teaspoon cinnamon

1/4 teaspoon powdered ginger

1/8 teaspoon vanilla extract

1/8 teaspoon cayenne pepper (or more!)

The Noodles

4 - 6 zucchini, spiralized

Blend all of the sauce ingredients together until creamy and smooth. Pour over noodles and enjoy!

CHAPTER 10

DESSERTS

SWEET DREAMS HEMP COOKIES

See photo at KristensRaw.com/photos.

Yield 1/2 cup cookie dough

> 1/4 cup *Raw Hemp Seed Butter* (see recipe, p. 61)
> 1/2 cup dried coconut, shredded & unsweetened
> 1/3 cup raisins
> 2 tablespoons raw agave nectar
> 1/4 teaspoon vanilla extract
> pinch Himalayan crystal salt
> 1/4 cup hemp seeds to roll the cookies in after making

Stir everything together in a bowl with a spoon (large bowl and spoon if you're making a double or triple batch). Then, take a moment and mash it together with your hands. Yes, it's sticky and gooey, but it's fun and you still have to roll them so you'll be getting sticky and gooey anyway.

Using about 1 tablespoon (or less) of the cookie dough, roll them into balls. Then, roll the cookies in the hemp seeds. Store these in the refrigerator or freezer.

Variation:

- Stir in 1 tablespoon of raw chocolate powder or raw carob powder

CHOCOLATE HEMP EXTRAVAGANCE

Yield one 8x8 glass baking dish

  2 cups dried coconut, shredded & unsweetened
  1 cup hemp seeds
  1/2 cup raw chocolate powder
  2 tablespoons hemp protein powder
  1/2 cup coconut oil
  1/2 cup raw agave nectar

Stir all of the ingredients together in a large bowl. Press into an 8x8 glass baking dish and place in the refrigerator to set for an hour or less. Cut into 12 or 16 treats and enjoy; or, have fun and use cookie cutters.

CURRANT HEMP RENDEZVOUS

Yield 1-cup cookie dough

Native to Australia, did you know that the macadamia tree was originally grown only for ornamental purposes? Macadamia nuts are filled with monounsaturated fat, which has been shown in study after study to be correlated with reducing heart disease and cancer.

1/2 cup macadamia nuts

1/2 cup hemp seeds

1/2 cup currants

1 tablespoon coconut oil

1 teaspoon vanilla extract

pinch Himalayan crystal salt

dash nutmeg

Grind the macadamia nuts in a food processor, fitted with the "S" blade, until coarsely ground. Add the remaining ingredients and process until thoroughly mixed together. Roll into cookie balls.

CAROB FENNEL HEMP TRUFFLES

Yield approximately 12 - 15 truffles

3/4 cup hemp seeds

1/3 cup raw carob powder

1/2 cup dried coconut, shredded & unsweetened

1/4 cup raw cacao nibs

3 tablespoons raw agave nectar

2 tablespoons coconut oil

1/2 teaspoon coconut extract

1/4 teaspoon ground fennel

dash Himalayan crystal salt

12 - 15 pecans for garnish to press on top of each truffle

Place all of the ingredients in your food processor, fitted with the "S" blade, and process until mixed thoroughly (approximately one minute). Roll the mixture into 1-tablespoon-size balls, flatten a little and gently press a pecan on top. Enjoy right away, or place them in the refrigerator (or freezer) until chilled.

Variation:

- Make a variety of truffles by rolling them in raw carob powder, raw chocolate powder, finely chopped nuts, or shredded unsweetened dried coconut

SUPERFOOD HEMP COOKIES

Yield 2 cups of batter

This is, hands down, one of my favorite Raw cookie recipes. I feel like a super hero when I'm eating these, and it's no wonder with all the super foods inside them!

1/3 cup *Raw Hemp Seed Butter* (see recipe, p. 61)

1/2 cup raw pecan butter*

1/2 cup dried coconut, shredded & unsweetened

1/2 cup raisins

3 tablespoons raw agave nectar

2 tablespoons hemp seeds

2 tablespoons goji berries

1 tablespoon coconut oil

1 tablespoon raw chocolate powder

1/4 teaspoon cinnamon

1/4 teaspoon maple extract

dash Himalayan crystal salt

Place all of the ingredients in a food processor, fitted with the "S" blade. Process until thoroughly mixed and "almost" creamy. Roll the cookies into balls using 1 tablespoon (more or less as you prefer) and enjoy!

* You can make this yourself by simply processing raw pecans in your food processor, fitted with the "S" blade, until it turns into butter. Or, you can find it in many health food stores or online.

CHOCOLATE CREAM VERVE-A-LICIOUS TART!

Yield one 9-inch tart

The first time I took this amazing dessert to a friend's party, it was devoured in minutes. Literally. I was asked for the recipe by every person there. I must say... IT IS AWESOME!

The Crust

> 1/3 cup raw cacao nibs
>
> 1 1/4 cups dried coconut, shredded & unsweetened
>
> 1 cup hemp seeds
>
> 1/4 teaspoon Himalayan crystal salt
>
> dash cayenne pepper
>
> 1/4 cup raw agave nectar
>
> 5 soft dates, pitted

The Filling

> 5 soft dates, pitted, soaked 20 minutes, drained
>
> 3/4 cup young Thai coconut water
>
> meat from one young Thai coconut (at least a 1/2 cup)
>
> 1/2 cup raw agave nectar
>
> 1 avocado, pitted and peeled
>
> 1 tablespoon green powder*
>
> 1 tablespoon hemp protein powder
>
> 3/4 cup raw chocolate powder
>
> 1 teaspoon maca powder (optional)
>
> 1/2 teaspoon vanilla extract

The Sweet Strawberry Coulis

> 1 (10oz) bag frozen strawberries, thawed (or fresh, destemmed)
>
> 1/4 cup raw agave nectar

The Crust Directions

Grind the cacao nibs in your food processor, fitted with the "S" blade, until they are broken up nicely into somewhat of a coarse powder. Add the coconut, hemp seeds, salt and cayenne, and process for a few seconds as you incorporate all of the ingredients together. Add the agave and dates and process until the mixture starts to stick together briefly when pressed together between your fingers.

Press the crust in to the tart pan until it's smoothly and firmly inside the pan. This crust is a little sticky, so using some coconut oil on you hands, or a tool used to press it in (spatula, for example), can help. Place the crust in the freezer while you make the filling.

The Filling Directions

Blend all of the ingredients until creamy. Pour the filling on top of the crust. Place the tart in the freezer for about 1 - 2 hours to set.

The Coulis Directions

Blend the ingredients together.

You can enjoy this tart right out of the freezer (or let it thaw a bit before eating), topped with Sweet Strawberry Coulis.

* As of this writing, my favorite brand is Vitamineral Green (visit KristensRaw.com/store for details), but new green powders are always being introduced and I experiment with many of them.

CINNAMON PEACH HEMP ICE CREAM

Yield 4 - 6 servings

> 2 cups peaches, pitted and chopped (or frozen and thawed peaches)
>
> 3/4 cup hemp seeds
>
> 1/2 cup raw agave nectar
>
> 1/2 cup young Thai coconut water
>
> 3/4 cup young Thai coconut meat
>
> 1/2 teaspoon cinnamon

Blend all of the ingredients until smooth and creamy. Pour into a shallow container (an 8x8 glass baking dish works well). Cover it and freeze overnight.

CINNAMON VANILLA HEMP CHEESECAKE

Yield one 8 or 9-inch cheesecake

The Crust

> 3/4 cup walnuts or pecans
>
> 1 1/2 cups hemp seeds
>
> 1/2 teaspoon cinnamon
>
> 1/8 teaspoon Himalayan crystal salt
>
> 1/2 cup raisins

The Filling

> 1 cup cashews, soaked 1 hour, drained and rinsed
>
> 1 cup macadamia nuts, soaked 1 hour, drained and rinsed
>
> 1 cup hemp seeds
>
> 1/2 cup raw agave nectar
>
> 5 soft dates, pitted
>
> 1/2 cup fresh lemon juice
>
> 1/4 cup water
>
> 2 tablespoons vanilla extract
>
> 2 1/2 teaspoons cinnamon

(continued)

pinch Himalayan crystal salt

2/3 cup coconut oil

2 tablespoons soy lecithin, optional

For the Crust

Place the walnuts or pecans in a food processor, fitted with the "S" blade, and process until coarsely ground. Add the hemp seeds, cinnamon and salt and process briefly. Add the raisins and process until the mixture begins to stick together when gently pressed between two of your fingers.

Press into the bottom of an 8 or 9-inch spring form pan. Place the crust in the freezer while you make the filling.

For the Filling

Blend all of the ingredients, except the coconut oil and soy lecithin, in a food processor until creamy (5 - 7 minutes). You may need to stop every couple of minutes to scrape down the sides.

Add the coconut oil and process to incorporate well. Add the soy lecithin and briefly process to incorporate. Pour the filling on top of the crust and smooth the top of it with an offset spatula.

You can freeze the cheesecake for a couple of hours or overnight. Then, let it thaw in your refrigerator (or on top of your counter) before serving. Cinnamon Vanilla Hemp Cheesecake will stay fresh for up to a week, when stored in an airtight container, in your refrigerator. Or, freeze it for up to six months.

CHOCOLATE PEPPERMINT HEMP CHEESECAKE

See photo at KristensRaw.com/photos.

Yield one 8 or 9-inch cheesecake

Chocolate peppermint has been one of my favorite flavor combinations since I was a little girl. I had to make a cheesecake to satisfy that craving. This is so good!

The Crust

1 cup walnuts

2 tablespoons raw cacao nibs

1 1/4 cups hemp seeds

1/8 teaspoon Himalayan crystal salt

2 teaspoons raw chocolate powder

1/4 teaspoon peppermint extract

1/4 teaspoon dried peppermint leaves

1/2 cup currants or raisins

The Filling

1 cup cashews, soaked 1 hour, drained and rinsed

1 cup macadamia nuts, soaked 1 hour, drained and rinsed

1 cup hemp seeds

1/2 cup raw dark (or blue) agave nectar*

(continued)

102

7 soft dates, pitted

1/2 cup fresh lemon juice

1/4 cup water

2 teaspoons peppermint extract

3/4 cup raw chocolate powder or raw carob powder

3/4 cup coconut oil

2 tablespoons soy lecithin, optional

For the Crust

Place the walnuts and cacao nibs in a food processor, fitted with the "S" blade, and process until coarsely ground. Add the hemp seeds, salt, chocolate powder, peppermint extract, and dried peppermint and process briefly to mix. Add the currants and process until the mixture begins to stick together when gently pressed between two of your fingers.

Press the crust mixture into the bottom of an 8 or 9-inch spring form pan. Place the crust in the freezer while you make the filling.

For the Filling

Blend all of the ingredients, except the coconut oil and soy lecithin, in a food processor until creamy (5 - 7 minutes). You may need to stop every couple of minutes to scrape down the sides.

Add the coconut oil and process to incorporate well. Add the soy lecithin and briefly process to incorporate. Pour the filling on top of the crust and smooth the top of it with an offset spatula.

You can freeze the cheesecake for a couple of hours or overnight. Then, let it thaw in your refrigerator (or on top of your counter) before serving. Chocolate Peppermint Hemp Cheesecake will stay fresh for up to a week, when stored in an airtight container, in your refrigerator. Or, freeze it for up to six months.

* I prefer Wholesome Sweetner's Organic Raw Blue Agave.

CHERRY CHOCOLATE BROWNIES

Yield 8x8 glass baking dish

This is sure to satisfy all of you Cherry Chocolate fans out there. I made these for a friend's birthday and he went CRAZY over them.

    1 1/2 cups dehydrated almond pulp, ground

    1 tablespoon lucuma powder*

    3 tablespoons raw chocolate powder

    1/4 cup hemp seeds

    1 teaspoon cherry extract

    1/4 cup raw agave nectar

    2 tablespoons extra virgin coconut oil

    3/4 cup dried cherries

Using your food processor, fitted with the "S" blade, pulse to briefly mix the almond pulp, lucuma, chocolate, and hemp seeds. Add the remaining ingredients and process until the mixture sticks together when gently pressed between two of your fingers.

Press the delicious mixture firmly into an 8x8 glass baking dish. Cut into squares and serve as is, or topped with Raw ice cream for extra indulgence.

* Available at NavitasNaturals.com.

SMILING GIRL FROZEN FUDGIES

Yield 1 cup

The perfect summertime treat. Ahhh, who am I kidding? These are perfect ANYTIME!

- 1/2 cup water
- 1/3 cup raw agave nectar
- 1 avocado, pitted and peeled
- 1/3 cup raw chocolate powder
- 1 tablespoon coconut butter
- 1 tablespoon coconut oil
- 1 tablespoon hemp protein powder
- 1/4 teaspoon almond extract

Blend all of the ingredients until smooth and pour into popsicle molds (or an ice cube tray for Smiling Girl Frozen Fudgie Bites) and freeze. Enjoy with a smile!

CHAPTER 11

BREAKFAST

EASY BRIGHT & LIGHT BREAKFAST

Yield 3 cups

Here is a delightful, light and easy breakfast recipe.

- 1 apple, cored and chopped
- 2 cups carrot, chopped
- 3 tablespoons hemp seeds
- 1 teaspoon fresh lemon juice
- 1/4 teaspoon maple extract
- 1/8 teaspoon cinnamon
- pinch Himalayan crystal salt
- tiny pinch nutmeg

Place all of the ingredients in a food processor, fitted with the "S" blade, and process until pureed to desired texture.

MOUNTAINEERS' HEARTY HEMP PANCAKES

Yield 2 cups batter, approximately 2 servings

    1/2 cup water
    1/2 cup hemp seeds
    2 tablespoons hemp protein powder
    1 banana, peeled
    1 apple, cored and chopped
    1/2 teaspoon cinnamon
    1/4 teaspoon vanilla extract
    1/4 teaspoon maple extract
    pinch nutmeg
    pinch Himalayan crystal salt
    1/2 cup flax meal*

In your blender, puree all of the ingredients, except the flax meal. Add the flax meal to the blender and briefly blend to mix.

Measure out (using a 1/4-cup) and spread the batter into pancakes on a dehydrator tray, fitted with a Paraflexx sheet. Dehydrate the pancakes at 130 degrees for 75 minutes. Lower the temperature to 105 degrees and continue dehydrating for about two more hours. Flip the pancakes onto the mesh dehydrator sheet and gently peel off the Paraflexx sheet. Continue dehydrating another 6 - 8 hours (or until your desired texture is achieved).

Store your pancakes in an airtight container in your refrigerator for up to five days. Before serving, you can warm them in the dehydrator for about 20 minutes at a temperature between 110 - 125 degrees. Serve with *Maple Hemp Syrup* (see recipe, p. 109).

* Grind 1/4 - 1/3 cup whole flax seeds to get this amount of flax meal.

MAPLE HEMP SYRUP

Yield 1/2 cup

This is a great, easy, and super delicious maple syrup that is actually Raw!

    1/2 cup raw dark (or blue) agave nectar*
    2 teaspoons maple extract
    1 tablespoon hemp oil

Stir all of the ingredients together in a bowl. Serve with *Mountaineers' Hearty Hemp Pancakes* (see recipe, p. 107) or over any fruit salad.

* I prefer Wholesome Sweetner's Organic Raw Blue Agave.

Breinigsville, PA USA
11 February 2010
232349BV00004B/89/P